POWER BI

Mastering DAX

for Advanced Data Modeling

Kiet Huynh

Table of Contents

CHAPTER I
Fundamentals of DAX

Part 1. Introduction to Data Analysis Expressions (DAX)

1.1. Understanding DAX Terminology

In the world of Power BI and data analysis, it's essential to speak the language, and Data Analysis Expressions (DAX) comes with its unique terminology that lays the foundation for all that follows. This section delves into the key concepts and terms you need to grasp to navigate the DAX landscape effectively.

Key DAX Terminology

1. Data Model: A data model is the foundational structure in Power BI that defines how your data is organized, related, and used in your reports and dashboards. It encompasses tables, relationships, and measures.

2. Table: In DAX, a table is a collection of related data organized in rows and columns. Tables are the building blocks of your data model and are used for various calculations and analyses.

3. Column: A column is a single attribute or field within a table that holds specific data. Columns can be used to store various types of data, such as text, numbers, dates, or Boolean values.

4. Row Context: Row context refers to the current row being evaluated in a table when performing calculations. It's crucial to understand row context to create context-aware DAX formulas.

5. Filter Context: Filter context is the set of filters applied to the data when a DAX formula is calculated. These filters can come from slicers, visuals, or other parts of the report, and they influence the results of calculations.

6. Measure: A measure is a DAX expression that performs calculations on your data model. Measures are used to aggregate and summarize data, providing valuable insights in your reports.

7. Calculated Column: A calculated column is a column in a table that you create using a DAX expression. It allows you to add new data to your model by defining custom calculations.

8. Function: DAX functions are pre-built operations that allow you to perform specific calculations. There are many DAX functions available, each serving a unique purpose.

9. Relationship: Relationships define how tables are connected in a data model. Understanding relationships is crucial for performing calculations that involve data from multiple tables.

10. Context Transition: Context transition is the process of switching between row context and filter context. It's a fundamental concept for creating complex DAX calculations.

By mastering these key DAX terminology, you'll be well-equipped to dive deeper into the world of data modeling and analysis with confidence. In the following chapters, we'll explore how these concepts are applied to solve real-world problems and unlock the full potential of Power BI.

1.2. DAX Data Types and Operators

In the realm of Data Analysis Expressions (DAX), a firm understanding of data types and operators is paramount. DAX is a formula language designed to perform calculations, and these calculations often involve data of various types. This section explores the intricacies of DAX data types and the operators that facilitate calculations in Power BI.

DAX Data Types

DAX recognizes several data types, each serving specific purposes in your calculations. Let's delve into the most common DAX data types:

1. Numeric Data Types:

  - Integer (Whole Number): Represents whole numbers without decimal places. Commonly used for counts or quantities.

  - Decimal: Handles numbers with decimal places, providing precision for more detailed calculations.

2. Text Data Type:

  - String: Used to store text values such as names, descriptions, or labels. Text data types are crucial for creating meaningful visuals and reports.

3. Date and Time Data Types:

  - Date: Stores calendar dates without time information. Dates are essential for time-based analysis and reporting.

  - Time: Represents time of day, typically without a date component. Useful for tracking time-specific events.

  - DateTime: Combines date and time information, making it suitable for timestamps and time-sensitive calculations.

4. Boolean Data Type:

   - Boolean: Booleans have only two possible values - True or False. They are indispensable for conditions and logical expressions in DAX.

5. Currency Data Type:

   - Currency: Specifically designed for handling monetary values, ensuring precision in financial calculations.

6. Percentage Data Type:

   - Percentage: Ideal for working with percentage values, simplifying the representation of proportions and ratios.

7. Whole Number Data Types:

   - Auto: Auto data types are dynamic and adapt to the specific value in the column, changing based on the data.

DAX Operators

DAX operators are the tools you use to perform calculations and comparisons. They allow you to combine, manipulate, and transform data. Here are the fundamental DAX operators:

1. Arithmetic Operators: Include addition (+), subtraction (-), multiplication (*), division (/), and others for numerical calculations.

2. Comparison Operators: Facilitate comparisons between values. Common comparison operators are equal to (=), not equal to (<>), greater than (>), and less than (<).

3. Logical Operators: Logical operators like AND, OR, and NOT are used to create complex conditions and expressions.

4. Text Operators: Text operators, such as concatenation (&), enable the manipulation of text values.

5. Data Type Conversion Operators: These operators help convert data types, ensuring compatibility for operations.

6. Table Operators: Operators like UNION, INTERSECT, and EXCEPT are used to manipulate tables, combining or extracting data.

7. Filter Operators: FILTER and ALL are filter operators that affect the filter context in DAX calculations.

Understanding DAX data types and operators is crucial for crafting effective calculations, measures, and formulas in Power BI. By leveraging the appropriate data types and operators, you can harness the full power of DAX for advanced data modeling and analysis.

1.3. DAX Syntax and Calculations

Understanding Data Analysis Expressions (DAX) syntax and calculations is essential for harnessing the full power of DAX in Power BI. DAX is a formula language that allows you to create custom calculations, measures, and calculations within your data model. In this section, we will explore the syntax and the fundamental concepts of DAX calculations.

DAX Formula Syntax

DAX formulas consist of a combination of functions, operators, and references to columns or tables within your data model. Here is the basic structure of a DAX formula:

```
```
=FunctionName([Column/Measure/Value], [Filter Criteria])
```
```

- FunctionName: This is the name of the DAX function that performs a specific calculation. DAX provides a wide range of functions for various tasks, from simple arithmetic to complex statistical analysis.

- Column/Measure/Value: This is the data that you want to operate on. It can be a column from a table, a measure you've created, or a specific value.

- Filter Criteria: Optional, this part allows you to apply filters to the data you're working with. It can be used for narrowing down the data you want to include in your calculation.

Basic DAX Functions

DAX includes a rich library of functions, each serving a specific purpose. Some of the fundamental DAX functions include:

- SUM: Used to add up values in a column.

- AVERAGE: Calculates the average of a column of values.

- COUNT: Counts the number of rows in a table or column.

- MIN/MAX: Find the minimum or maximum value in a column.

- IF: Allows you to create conditional calculations based on a specified condition.

Context in DAX Calculations

DAX calculations work within a specific context, which can be row context or filter context. Understanding context is crucial for writing effective DAX formulas.

- Row Context: When a DAX formula operates within the context of a specific row, it considers the data in that row for calculations. This is useful for creating calculations that depend on individual data points.

- Filter Context: Filter context occurs when filters are applied to your data, such as through slicers or visuals. DAX formulas respect these filters and calculate results based on the filtered data.

Measures and Calculated Columns

DAX allows you to create two primary types of calculations: measures and calculated columns.

- Measures: Measures are calculated values that provide a single result, typically an aggregation of data. They are used in visualizations to summarize data and provide key insights.

- Calculated Columns: Calculated columns add new data to your data model by defining custom calculations for each row. These columns are computed during data refresh and can be used like any other column in your tables.

Creating Effective DAX Formulas

To create effective DAX formulas, it's essential to understand the problem you're trying to solve, choose the right DAX functions, and consider the context in which your calculations will operate. Start with simple calculations and gradually build more complex formulas as needed.

In this section, we've explored the foundational concepts of DAX syntax and calculations. The ability to write effective DAX formulas is a critical skill for advanced data modeling in Power BI. As we move forward in this book, we will dive deeper into real-world scenarios and advanced techniques that leverage DAX to its fullest potential.

Part 2. DAX Functions and Calculated Columns

2.1. An Overview of DAX Functions

Data Analysis Expressions (DAX) functions are the building blocks of your calculations in Power BI. DAX functions perform a wide range of operations, from simple arithmetic to complex statistical analyses. In this section, we will provide an in-depth overview of DAX functions, their categories, and how to use them effectively in your data modeling journey.

Understanding DAX Functions

DAX functions are predefined formulas designed to perform specific calculations, transformations, and aggregations on your data. They simplify the process of creating custom measures and calculated columns, allowing you to extract valuable insights from your data.

Categories of DAX Functions

DAX functions can be categorized into several key groups, each serving a distinct purpose. Here are the primary categories of DAX functions:

1. Aggregation Functions: These functions are used to summarize and aggregate data. Common aggregation functions include:

   - SUM: Adds up values in a column.

   - AVERAGE: Calculates the average of a column.

   - MIN/MAX: Find the minimum or maximum value in a column.

2. Filter Functions: Filter functions allow you to create calculations based on specific criteria or conditions. Notable filter functions include:

- FILTER: Filters a table or expression based on a condition.

- ALL: Removes filters from a table or columns, enabling broader analysis.

3. Information Functions: Information functions provide metadata about your data model, tables, and columns. Examples include:

  - COUNTROWS: Counts the number of rows in a table.

  - ISBLANK/ISNUMBER/ISTEXT: Check the data type of a value.

4. Time Intelligence Functions: These functions are tailored for time-based analysis. Time intelligence functions are crucial for creating time-related calculations and comparisons.

5. Text Functions: Text functions manipulate text values, making them essential for creating custom labels and descriptions in your reports.

6. Math and Trigonometry Functions: Mathematical functions help you perform complex calculations, including trigonometric operations.

7. Statistical Functions: Statistical functions enable advanced statistical analysis, such as calculating standard deviations, variance, and regression.

8. Logical Functions: Logical functions handle conditional calculations and return True or False values. They are vital for decision-making and branching logic.

Function Syntax and Usage

Each DAX function has a specific syntax, which consists of the function name, arguments, and optional parameters. Understanding the syntax is crucial for using DAX functions effectively.

In this section, we will explore examples of DAX functions and how to apply them to real-world scenarios. We'll cover simple use cases and progressively move to more complex calculations, ensuring that you can harness the full potential of DAX functions in your data modeling journey.

By the end of this section, you will have a solid foundation in DAX functions, enabling you to leverage these tools to perform a wide range of calculations and create meaningful insights from your data.

2.2. Using Calculated Columns for Data Enrichment

In the world of data modeling with Power BI, calculated columns are a powerful tool that allows you to enrich your data by creating custom columns based on calculated expressions. This section explores the concept of calculated columns, why they are essential, and how to use them effectively to enhance your data model.

What Are Calculated Columns?

Calculated columns are virtual columns that you add to your data model. Unlike regular columns that are part of your data source, calculated columns are created within Power BI, and they contain values generated by DAX expressions. These expressions can be as simple as basic arithmetic operations or as complex as advanced statistical calculations.

Why Use Calculated Columns for Data Enrichment?

Calculated columns offer several advantages for data enrichment:

1. Custom Data Transformations: Calculated columns allow you to transform your data in ways that are not possible with your original data source. You can create new attributes, derive additional information, or standardize data values.

2. Enhanced Analytics: By enriching your data with calculated columns, you enable more sophisticated analysis and reporting. These custom columns provide the foundation for creating meaningful visuals and deriving deeper insights.

3. Consistency: Calculated columns ensure data consistency across your entire data model. You can implement business rules, apply data validation, or handle data cleansing tasks to ensure the quality and reliability of your data.

Using Calculated Columns Effectively

To use calculated columns effectively for data enrichment, follow these key steps:

1. Identify Enrichment Goals: Determine what specific enhancements or transformations are required for your data. This could involve creating new attributes, aggregating data, or standardizing values.

2. Write DAX Expressions: Craft DAX expressions that define how your calculated columns will be generated. These expressions should be precise and tailored to your data enrichment goals.

3. Test and Validate: Always test your calculated columns to ensure they produce the desired results. Check for accuracy and consistency, especially in scenarios involving complex calculations.

4. Performance Considerations: Be mindful of performance implications. Calculated columns are computed during data refresh, and creating too many or overly complex calculated columns can impact performance.

Examples of Data Enrichment

Let's look at a few practical examples of using calculated columns for data enrichment:

1. Age Calculation: You can create a calculated column to determine the age of customers based on their birthdate.

2. Categorization: Create calculated columns to categorize products, customers, or sales data into specific groups for easier analysis.

3. Currency Conversion: If your data involves multiple currencies, calculated columns can be used to convert all values to a common currency for consistent reporting.

4. Data Standardization: Implement calculated columns to standardize data formats, such as dates, phone numbers, or addresses.

By effectively utilizing calculated columns for data enrichment, you can elevate the quality and analytical capabilities of your Power BI data model. Calculated columns offer flexibility and customization, making them a valuable asset in your data modeling toolkit.

In this section, we will explore the use of calculated columns to enrich your data in Power BI. Calculated columns allow you to create new columns in your tables that derive values from existing data, providing additional insights for your reports. Let's consider an example to illustrate this concept.

Illustrative Example: Using Calculated Columns for Data Enrichment

Scenario:

You are working with a sales dataset in Power BI. You have a "Sales" table containing information about sales transactions, including the "Product," "Quantity Sold," and "Price." You want to enrich this data by creating a calculated column for "Total Sales Amount" for each transaction.

Data Structure:

- Sales Table:

  - Columns: "Transaction ID," "Product," "Quantity Sold," "Price"

Calculated Column:

1. Calculating Total Sales Amount:

   - You want to create a calculated column that calculates the total sales amount for each transaction by multiplying the "Quantity Sold" and "Price."

   Custom Calculated Column Formula:

```DAX
Total Sales Amount = 'Sales'[Quantity Sold] * 'Sales'[Price]
```

Data Enrichment:

- By creating the "Total Sales Amount" calculated column, you enrich the dataset with a new column that automatically calculates the total sales amount for each transaction.

- This calculated column allows you to perform aggregations, create visualizations, and gain insights into your sales data more efficiently.

Example Use Case:

- With the "Total Sales Amount" calculated column in place, you can easily create visuals and measures to analyze total sales, average sales, or any other sales-related metrics in your reports without the need to recompute the values in real-time.

This example demonstrates how calculated columns can be used for data enrichment, providing valuable insights and simplifying the analysis of your data in Power BI.

2.3. Combining Functions for Complex Calculations

In the realm of data modeling and analysis, complex calculations often require combining multiple DAX functions to achieve specific outcomes. This section explores the art of combining DAX functions to solve intricate data challenges and unlock deeper insights within your Power BI projects.

The Power of Combining DAX Functions

DAX functions serve as the building blocks of your calculations in Power BI, and they can be incredibly powerful when combined strategically. By combining functions, you can address a wide range of analytical needs, from transforming raw data to performing advanced statistical analyses.

Principles of Combining DAX Functions

Combining DAX functions effectively involves several key principles:

1. Function Nesting: DAX functions can be nested inside one another, allowing you to create complex expressions. For example, you can use the result of one function as an input to another.

2. Order of Operations: Understanding the order in which DAX functions are evaluated is crucial. Some functions may rely on prior calculations or filters applied to the data.

3. Context Handling: Be mindful of row context and filter context, as they influence how DAX functions operate. Combining functions should respect the context in which they are used.

Real-World Examples

To illustrate the power of combining DAX functions, let's explore a few real-world examples:

1. Dynamic Segmentation: Combine filter functions, aggregation functions, and logical functions to dynamically segment data based on user-selected criteria, allowing for interactive analysis.

2. Advanced Time Intelligence: Create complex time intelligence calculations by combining functions to calculate rolling averages, year-to-date measures, or cumulative totals.

3. Predictive Analytics: Utilize statistical functions and logical functions to perform predictive analytics, such as forecasting future sales based on historical data.

4. Advanced Financial Modeling: Combine functions to build advanced financial models, calculate net present value, internal rate of return, and other financial metrics.

Challenges and Best Practices

While combining DAX functions can be powerful, it can also introduce challenges such as performance considerations, complexity, and potential errors. It's essential to follow best practices when working with complex DAX calculations, including:

1. Testing and Validation: Always thoroughly test complex calculations to ensure they provide accurate and reliable results.

2. Documentation: Document your complex DAX calculations for future reference and collaboration with other team members.

3. Performance Optimization: Be mindful of performance implications when combining functions. Some calculations may require optimization to maintain efficient report performance.

4. Iterative Functions: Understand when to use iterative functions and their impact on performance, especially when dealing with large datasets.

By mastering the art of combining DAX functions for complex calculations, you'll have the ability to unlock deeper insights, create more sophisticated reports, and address a wide range of data modeling challenges in Power BI.

In this section, we will explore the power of combining DAX functions to perform complex calculations in Power BI. By chaining and nesting functions, you can create sophisticated calculations that provide deeper insights into your data. Let's consider an example to illustrate this concept.

Illustrative Example: Combining Functions for Complex Calculations

Scenario:

Imagine you are working with a financial dataset that includes information about stock prices. You have a "Stock Prices" table with columns like "Date" and "Closing Price." You want to create a calculated measure that calculates the average closing price over a moving three-day window.

Data Structure:

- Stock Prices Table:

  - Columns: "Date," "Closing Price"

Complex Calculation:

1. Calculating Moving Average:

   - You want to create a calculated measure, "Moving Average," that calculates the average closing price over a three-day moving window.

Custom DAX Measure Formula:

```DAX
Moving Average =
AVERAGEX(
```

```
    FILTER(
        'Stock Prices',
        'Stock Prices'[Date] >= EARLIER('Stock Prices'[Date]) - 2 && 'Stock Prices'[Date] <= EARLIER('Stock Prices'[Date])
    ),
    'Stock Prices'[Closing Price]
)
```

Explanation:

- In this calculation, we use the AVERAGEX function to calculate the average of a filtered table.

- The FILTER function is used to filter the "Stock Prices" table to include only the rows from the current date and the previous two days (a three-day moving window).

- We calculate the average of the "Closing Price" column within this filtered table, giving us the moving average.

Use Case:

- The "Moving Average" measure can now be used in your reports and visualizations to track the three-day moving average of stock prices.

- This allows you to identify trends and patterns more easily, which can be valuable for financial analysis.

This example demonstrates how combining DAX functions can be used to perform complex calculations in Power BI, enabling you to gain deeper insights into your data and create more informative reports.

Part 3. DAX Measures and Key Performance Indicators (KPIs)

3.1. Creating Measures for Aggregations

Measures in Power BI are the backbone of your data analysis and reporting. They allow you to perform calculations, aggregations, and summarize data in a way that provides meaningful insights. In this section, we will explore the art of creating measures for aggregations and learn how to make the most of this essential feature in Power BI.

Understanding Measures in Power BI

Measures in Power BI are dynamic calculations that aggregate data based on user-defined expressions. Unlike calculated columns, measures do not add new columns to your data model but instead provide a way to generate results on the fly, depending on the context of your visualizations and user interactions.

Why Use Measures for Aggregations?

Measures offer several advantages for aggregating data:

1. Flexibility: Measures are highly flexible and adapt to the context of your reports. They adjust to filters, slicers, and user interactions, providing real-time insights.

2. Reusability: Measures can be reused across different visualizations and reports, promoting consistency and efficiency in your data analysis.

3. Consistency: Measures ensure that calculations are consistent throughout your reports, reducing the risk of errors or inconsistencies in your data analysis.

Creating Effective Measures

To create effective measures for aggregations, follow these key steps:

1. Identify Aggregation Goals: Determine what specific aggregations are required for your data analysis. Are you looking to calculate sums, averages, counts, or more complex metrics?

2. Write DAX Expressions: Craft DAX expressions that define how your measures will perform aggregations. Expressions should be precise and tailored to your aggregation goals.

3. Test and Validate: Always test your measures to ensure they provide the desired results. Validate their accuracy and consistency in various scenarios.

4. Naming Conventions: Follow naming conventions for measures to make them easily identifiable and maintainable. Clear and meaningful names enhance the user experience.

Real-World Examples

Let's explore practical examples of creating measures for aggregations:

1. Total Sales: Create a measure that calculates the total sales in your dataset. This measure can be used in various reports and visuals to display overall sales.

2. Average Order Value: Calculate the average order value by dividing total sales by the number of orders. This measure helps you understand customer spending patterns.

3. Customer Retention Rate: Develop a measure to determine the customer retention rate by analyzing data over time. This KPI provides insights into customer loyalty.

4. Churn Rate: Create a measure to calculate the churn rate by examining customer attrition. Churn rate is vital for customer relationship management.

Challenges and Best Practices

While creating measures for aggregations, consider best practices to ensure their effectiveness:

1. Data Granularity: Be aware of data granularity, as it affects the accuracy of your measures. Ensure that your data model is properly structured.

2. Performance Optimization: Monitor the performance of your measures, especially with large datasets. Implement optimization techniques when necessary.

3. Documentation: Document your measures, including their purpose, calculations, and any dependencies. Clear documentation supports collaboration and knowledge sharing.

By mastering the art of creating measures for aggregations, you'll have the ability to extract valuable insights, answer critical business questions, and present data-driven findings in a visually compelling manner in Power BI.

In this section, we will delve into creating DAX measures for aggregations in Power BI. Measures allow you to perform calculations on your data to derive meaningful insights. Let's explore a real-world scenario to illustrate this concept.

Illustrative Example: Creating Measures for Aggregations

Scenario:

Imagine you are managing a sales dataset for an e-commerce business. You have a "Sales" table with columns like "Order Date," "Product," "Quantity Sold," and "Revenue." You want to create DAX measures to analyze the total revenue and total quantity sold for different products.

Data Structure:

- Sales Table:

  - Columns: "Order Date," "Product," "Quantity Sold," "Revenue"

DAX Measures:

1. Total Revenue:

   - You want to create a measure, "Total Revenue," to calculate the sum of revenue across all sales transactions.

   Custom DAX Measure Formula:

```DAX
Total Revenue = SUM('Sales'[Revenue])
```

2. Total Quantity Sold:

   - You also want to create a measure, "Total Quantity Sold," to calculate the sum of quantity sold for all products.

   Custom DAX Measure Formula:


   ```DAX

   Total Quantity Sold = SUM('Sales'[Quantity Sold])

   ```


Explanation:

- The "Total Revenue" measure uses the SUM function to sum up the "Revenue" column in the "Sales" table, giving you the total revenue generated.

- The "Total Quantity Sold" measure similarly uses the SUM function to sum up the "Quantity Sold" column in the "Sales" table, providing you with the total quantity of products sold.

Use Case:

- These measures can be employed in your reports and dashboards to assess the overall performance of your e-commerce business, compare product sales, and identify trends in revenue and quantity sold.

This example demonstrates how creating DAX measures for aggregations in Power BI can provide you with a deeper understanding of your data, enabling you to make informed business decisions and visualize your data effectively.

3.2. Utilizing DAX for KPI Definitions

Key Performance Indicators (KPIs) are essential for monitoring and evaluating the performance of your business or organization. In this section, we will explore how to utilize Data Analysis Expressions (DAX) to define and measure KPIs effectively within your Power BI reports, enabling data-driven decision-making.

Understanding KPIs in Power BI

KPIs are quantifiable metrics that represent critical aspects of your business or project. They serve as performance benchmarks, helping you assess progress and make informed decisions. Power BI provides a framework for defining and visualizing KPIs, and DAX plays a central role in their calculation.

Why Use DAX for KPI Definitions?

Utilizing DAX for KPI definitions offers several advantages:

1. Flexibility: DAX allows you to define custom KPIs tailored to your specific business needs. You can adapt KPIs as your business evolves.

2. Integration: DAX seamlessly integrates with Power BI visuals, enabling you to present KPIs in a visually compelling and interactive manner.

3. Real-Time Updates: DAX-driven KPIs update in real-time based on user interactions, filters, or data changes, providing immediate insights.

Creating Effective DAX-Driven KPIs

To create effective KPIs using DAX, follow these key steps:

1. Define KPI Goals: Clearly define the goals and objectives of the KPI. What aspect of your business or project are you measuring, and what is the target or threshold for success?

2. Design DAX Calculations: Craft DAX calculations that align with your KPI goals. These calculations should be precise, taking into account the data context and desired outcomes.

3. Visual Representation: Select appropriate visuals to present your KPIs. Power BI offers various visualizations, including cards, gauges, and tables, to effectively display KPIs.

4. User Interaction: Configure user interactions to allow users to drill down or explore the factors contributing to KPI performance.

Real-World Examples

Let's explore practical examples of utilizing DAX for KPI definitions:

1. Sales Growth Rate: Define a KPI that calculates the year-over-year growth rate in sales. This KPI provides insights into revenue trends.

2. Customer Churn Rate: Create a KPI that measures customer attrition, helping you monitor and reduce customer churn.

3. Profit Margin: Define a KPI that calculates the profit margin, allowing you to assess the profitability of your products or services.

4. Service Level Agreement (SLA) Compliance: Develop a KPI that assesses the compliance of your customer support team with SLAs, ensuring timely responses to customer inquiries.

Challenges and Best Practices

When utilizing DAX for KPI definitions, consider challenges and best practices:

1. Data Quality: Ensure data quality and consistency, as KPIs are highly dependent on accurate data.

2. Goal Setting: Set realistic and meaningful KPI goals that align with your business objectives.

3. Performance Optimization: Optimize KPI calculations to maintain report performance, especially when dealing with large datasets.

4. Documentation: Document your KPIs and their definitions to enhance collaboration and understanding.

By effectively utilizing DAX for KPI definitions, you'll have the ability to track and assess critical aspects of your business or project, enabling data-driven decision-making and performance monitoring in Power BI.

Let's provide some illustrative examples to help you visualize the use of DAX (Data Analysis Expressions) in Power BI. These examples will demonstrate how DAX can be applied to real-world scenarios:

Example 1: Calculating Total Sales

Suppose you have a dataset containing sales data with columns for dates and sales amounts. You want to calculate the total sales for a specific period using DAX.

DAX Formula:

```
Total Sales = SUM(SalesTable[SalesAmount])
```

In this example, the `SUM` function is used to add up the values in the "SalesAmount" column of the "SalesTable." The resulting measure, "Total Sales," will dynamically calculate the total sales amount for the selected context (such as a specific date range) when used in a Power BI visual.

Example 2: Calculating Year-to-Date Sales

You want to calculate the year-to-date (YTD) sales, which is the sum of sales from the beginning of the current year up to the selected date.

DAX Formula:

```
YTD Sales = TOTALYTD(SUM(SalesTable[SalesAmount]), 'DateTable'[Date])
```

In this case, the `TOTALYTD` function is used to calculate the YTD sales. It takes the total sales amount from the "SalesTable" and applies a YTD calculation based on the 'DateTable' date column. This measure will dynamically show the YTD sales amount for the chosen period.

Example 3: Calculating Monthly Growth Rate

You want to determine the monthly growth rate of sales, which is the percentage change in sales from one month to the next.

DAX Formula:
```

Monthly Growth Rate = DIVIDE(

        SUM(SalesTable[SalesAmount]),

        CALCULATE(

        SUM(SalesTable[SalesAmount]),

        DATEADD('DateTable'[Date], -1, MONTH)

        )

    ) - 1

```

In this example, the `DIVIDE` function calculates the growth rate by dividing the total sales amount for the current month by the total sales amount for the previous month. The `-1` argument in `DATEADD` helps you retrieve the data for the previous month.

Example 4: Calculating Customer Retention Rate

You're interested in measuring customer retention by calculating the percentage of customers who made repeat purchases within a specific time frame.

DAX Formula:

```
Customer Retention Rate = DIVIDE(
        COUNTROWS(SalesTable),
        CALCULATE(
          COUNTROWS(SalesTable),
          FILTER(SalesTable, [SalesDate] >= EARLIER([SalesDate]) - 365)
        )
      )
```

In this instance, the `DIVIDE` function is used to calculate the retention rate. It divides the count of customers making purchases within the last 365 days by the total count of customers, providing a retention rate.

Illustrative Example: Utilizing DAX for KPI Definitions

Scenario:

Imagine you are managing a retail business, and you want to monitor the performance of your stores using KPIs. You have a "Sales" table with columns like "Store," "Revenue," and "Target Revenue." You want to define KPIs to measure whether each store has met its revenue target.

Data Structure:

- Sales Table:

  - Columns: "Store," "Revenue," "Target Revenue"

DAX Measures:

1. KPI: Revenue vs. Target:

   - You want to create a KPI that measures the performance of each store against its revenue target.

Custom DAX Measure Formula:

```DAX
Revenue vs. Target =
VAR ActualRevenue = SUM('Sales'[Revenue])
VAR TargetRevenue = SUM('Sales'[Target Revenue])
RETURN
IF(ISBLANK(ActualRevenue) || ISBLANK(TargetRevenue), BLANK(),
   IF(ActualRevenue >= TargetRevenue, "Met Target", "Missed Target"))
```

Explanation:

- The "Revenue vs. Target" measure calculates the actual revenue and target revenue for each store. It then compares the actual revenue to the target revenue and returns "Met Target" if the store met its target or "Missed Target" if it didn't.

Use Case:

- By utilizing this KPI, you can easily assess whether each store has achieved its revenue target. You can visualize this data on a dashboard, making it straightforward to identify stores that are performing well and those that need attention.

This example demonstrates how to leverage DAX for KPI definitions, allowing you to evaluate your business's performance against predefined targets, making data-driven decisions and monitoring key aspects of your organization's success.

These examples demonstrate how DAX can be applied to perform calculations and aggregations in Power BI. DAX allows you to create custom measures and calculated columns to analyze and visualize your data effectively for various business scenarios.

3.3. Implementing Time-Intelligent Measures

In the world of data modeling and analysis, understanding time-related data is crucial for making informed decisions. This section delves into the implementation of time-intelligent measures using Data Analysis Expressions (DAX) in Power BI. Time-intelligent measures help you analyze trends, patterns, and performance over time, enabling you to gain valuable insights.

The Significance of Time-Intelligent Measures

Time-intelligent measures allow you to perform calculations that take into account the temporal dimension of your data. These measures are particularly valuable when you need to understand changes, seasonality, or trends over time. Whether you are dealing with daily sales, monthly expenses, or yearly performance, time-intelligent measures are indispensable.

Key Concepts in Time-Intelligent Measures

Before we delve into practical examples, it's essential to understand key concepts in time-intelligent measures:

1. Date Tables: A date table is fundamental for time-based calculations. It provides the necessary context for time intelligence functions in DAX.

2. Time Intelligence Functions: DAX offers a rich library of time intelligence functions that enable you to perform calculations across various time periods. Functions like TOTALYTD, SAMEPERIODLASTYEAR, and DATESYTD are invaluable for these calculations.

3. Custom Calendar: In some scenarios, you may need to work with custom calendars, such as fiscal years or academic years. DAX allows you to implement custom calendars for precise time analysis.

Creating Time-Intelligent Measures

To create effective time-intelligent measures, follow these key steps:

1. Define the Time Period: Determine the time period you want to analyze. It could be daily, monthly, quarterly, or custom periods based on your business requirements.

2. Select the Time Frame: Decide on the specific timeframe you want to analyze, such as year-to-date, quarter-to-date, or any other relevant period.

3. Utilize Time Intelligence Functions: Leverage DAX time intelligence functions to create measures that aggregate and compare data over time.

4. Visualization: Choose appropriate visuals, such as line charts, bar charts, or sparklines, to represent time-intelligent measures effectively.

Practical Examples

Let's explore practical examples of implementing time-intelligent measures:

1. Year-to-Date Sales: Create a measure that calculates the year-to-date sales, allowing you to monitor the cumulative sales performance throughout the year.

2. Quarterly Growth: Develop a measure that assesses quarterly growth by comparing current quarter data with the previous quarter. This measure helps you track business expansion.

3. Moving Averages: Calculate moving averages to identify trends and smooth out fluctuations in your data, providing a clearer view of long-term patterns.

4. Seasonal Analysis: Implement measures that perform seasonal analysis by comparing data from the same season in different years. This is valuable for businesses with seasonal trends.

Challenges and Best Practices

When implementing time-intelligent measures, consider challenges and best practices:

1. Data Granularity: Ensure consistent data granularity in your date table to maintain accurate time analysis.

2. Performance Optimization: Monitor the performance of time-intelligent measures, especially with large datasets. Optimize calculations as needed.

3. Custom Calendars: If you're working with custom calendars, ensure they align with your business's fiscal or operational cycle.

4. Documentation: Document your time-intelligent measures and their calculations for future reference and collaboration.

In this section, we will delve into how to implement time-intelligent measures in Power BI using Data Analysis Expressions (DAX). Time-intelligent measures allow you to analyze data over different time periods while considering the context of your analysis.

Illustrative Example: Implementing Time-Intelligent Measures

Scenario:

Suppose you manage an e-commerce business, and you want to track sales trends over time. You have a "Sales" table with columns like "Date," "Revenue," and "Units Sold." You aim to create time-intelligent measures to analyze trends and compare them with previous periods.

Data Structure:

- Sales Table:

  - Columns: "Date," "Revenue," "Units Sold"

DAX Measures:

1. Year-over-Year (YoY) Sales Growth:

   - You want to measure the growth in sales revenue compared to the previous year.

Custom DAX Measure Formula:

```DAX
YoY Sales Growth =
CALCULATE([Total Revenue], SAMEPERIODLASTYEAR('Sales'[Date]))
```

2. Rolling 3-Month Average Revenue:

   - You want to calculate a rolling average of revenue over the past three months.

Custom DAX Measure Formula:

```DAX
3-Month Avg Revenue =
AVERAGEX(
    DATESINPERIOD('Sales'[Date], MAX('Sales'[Date]), -3, MONTH),
    [Revenue]
)
```

Explanation:

- The "YoY Sales Growth" measure uses the SAMEPERIODLASTYEAR function to compare the total revenue for the current year with the previous year, providing insights into year-over-year growth.

- The "3-Month Avg Revenue" measure calculates a rolling three-month average by considering the last three months' revenue data. It provides a smoother view of revenue trends over time.

Use Case:

- By applying these time-intelligent measures, you can effectively track sales growth year-over-year and visualize rolling averages of revenue. This empowers you to identify seasonality, trends, and variations in your business's performance, enabling informed decision-making.

These time-intelligent measures are essential for understanding how your business performs over different time periods, helping you make data-driven decisions and uncover insights to drive success.

By mastering the implementation of time-intelligent measures using DAX, you'll have the ability to uncover valuable insights, track trends, and make informed decisions based on the temporal dimension of your data. Time-intelligent measures are an indispensable tool for time-based data analysis in Power BI.

CHAPTER II
Data Modeling Strategies

Part 4. Efficient Data Model Design

4.1. Normalization vs. Denormalization

Efficient data model design is at the core of successful Power BI projects. One of the key decisions in data modeling is whether to normalize or denormalize the data structure. This section explores the concepts of normalization and denormalization and provides guidance on when to use each approach.

Understanding Normalization

Normalization is a database design technique that aims to reduce data redundancy and improve data integrity. It involves organizing data into separate tables, each with a specific purpose and minimal duplication of information. Normalized databases follow a set of rules called normal forms.

Advantages of Normalization:

1. Data Consistency: Normalization reduces data anomalies and inconsistencies by storing data in a structured, standardized format.

2. Efficient Updates: Updating data in a normalized database is more efficient since changes are made in one place, reducing the risk of data inconsistencies.

3. Saves Storage Space: Normalization typically requires less storage space because data is stored more efficiently.

Example of Normalization:

Suppose you have a database for an e-commerce platform. You may normalize the data by having separate tables for customers, products, orders, and order items. This minimizes redundant customer and product information across multiple orders.

Understanding Denormalization

Denormalization, on the other hand, is the process of intentionally introducing redundancy into a database design to improve query performance. It simplifies data retrieval by reducing the need for complex joins between tables.

Advantages of Denormalization:

1. Improved Query Performance: Denormalization can lead to faster query execution, as it reduces the number of joins required.

2. Simplified Reporting: For reporting purposes, denormalized structures can be more straightforward and easier to work with.

3. Aggregations: Denormalization is often used when pre-aggregating data, which is beneficial for analytical purposes.

Example of Denormalization:

In a reporting database, customer information may be denormalized into the order table. This makes it easier to retrieve customer details when analyzing order data, even if it means some customer information is duplicated.

When to Use Normalization vs. Denormalization

The choice between normalization and denormalization depends on your specific use case:

1. Normalization is suitable when data integrity and consistency are top priorities, such as in transactional systems where updates and data accuracy are critical.

2. Denormalization is ideal when query performance and reporting are the main concerns, such as in data warehousing and analytical scenarios where complex joins can slow down analysis.

Finding the Right Balance

In practice, many data models strike a balance between normalization and denormalization. This approach is often referred to as "controlled denormalization." It aims to provide the advantages of both approaches by carefully denormalizing specific parts of the data model for performance while keeping the core data in normalized form.

Example of Controlled Denormalization:

A data warehouse may denormalize some dimensions for faster query performance while keeping the fact tables normalized to maintain data accuracy.

By understanding the trade-offs between normalization and denormalization and applying these techniques judiciously, you can design a data model in Power BI that meets your specific business requirements, ensuring data integrity, query performance, and effective reporting.

4.2. Handling Slowly Changing Dimensions (SCDs)

In the world of data modeling, Slowly Changing Dimensions (SCDs) are a common challenge that data professionals face. This section explores the concept of SCDs, the strategies to handle them effectively, and provides real-world examples to illustrate the process.

Understanding Slowly Changing Dimensions

Slowly Changing Dimensions refer to attributes in a data model that change over time. These changes may occur at varying speeds, and it's crucial to manage and track them accurately to maintain data quality.

Types of SCDs:

1. Type 1 SCD: In this type, the old data is simply overwritten with new data. There's no historical tracking of changes.

2. Type 2 SCD: Here, a new row is added to the dimension table to represent the new data, while the old data remains unchanged. This allows historical tracking.

3. Type 3 SCD: In a Type 3 SCD, limited history is maintained, typically using separate columns to represent the old and new values.

Handling SCDs in Power BI

Handling SCDs effectively in Power BI involves defining strategies for managing changing dimension attributes. The choice of strategy depends on the specific SCD type and business requirements.

Illustrative Example: Type 2 SCD

Let's consider a scenario where you have a product dimension table in Power BI, and you want to track changes in product attributes over time. This is a typical Type 2 SCD scenario.

Step 1: Initial State

- Your product dimension table contains the initial product attributes.

- Each product has a unique identifier.

Step 2: Change Occurs

- One of the products changes its attributes. For instance, the product name is updated from "Product A" to "Updated Product A."

Step 3: Handling the Change

- To handle this change as a Type 2 SCD, a new row is added to the product dimension table with the updated attributes.

- The original product row remains in the table to maintain historical data.

Step 4: Historical Tracking

- The product dimension table now contains two rows for the same product, representing its historical changes.

- You can create a DAX measure or calculated column that selects the appropriate product attributes based on the desired time frame, ensuring accurate historical reporting.

Choosing the Right SCD Strategy

When handling SCDs, it's important to select the appropriate strategy based on your specific business requirements. Type 2 SCDs are commonly used for maintaining historical data while Type 1 SCDs are suitable when historical tracking is unnecessary.

Additional Strategies for SCDs:

- Type 3 SCDs can be implemented using separate columns for current and previous values.

- Hybrid approaches may also be used, combining different SCD types for specific attributes in the same dimension.

By mastering the handling of Slowly Changing Dimensions in Power BI, you'll be able to maintain data quality, track historical changes, and create accurate reports and analyses that reflect the evolving nature of your data. Effective SCD management is crucial for a robust data model in Power BI.

4.3. Managing Model Relationships

Effective data model design in Power BI relies heavily on managing relationships between tables. In this section, we will explore the critical aspects of managing model relationships, including the types of relationships, cardinality, and best practices.

Understanding Model Relationships

Model relationships in Power BI establish connections between tables, enabling users to navigate and analyze data seamlessly. Relationships can be one-to-one, one-to-many, or many-to-one, and they are fundamental to creating meaningful reports and dashboards.

Types of Model Relationships:

1. One-to-One (1:1): A single value in one table is related to a single value in another table. For example, a relationship between an Employee table and a Department table.

2. One-to-Many (1:N): A single value in one table is related to multiple values in another table. This is the most common relationship type, such as a relationship between a Sales table and a Product table.

3. Many-to-One (N:1): Multiple values in one table are related to a single value in another table. This is essentially the reverse of a one-to-many relationship.

Cardinality and Cross Filtering

Understanding the cardinality of relationships is essential. Cardinality defines how many records in the related table match each record in the primary table. Additionally, cross-filtering behavior plays a crucial role, determining how filter context flows between related tables.

Illustrative Example: One-to-Many Relationship

Let's consider a scenario where you have a Sales table and a Product table. You want to create a one-to-many relationship between these tables to analyze sales data by product.

Step 1: Creating the Relationship

- Establish a one-to-many relationship between the Sales table and the Product table, connecting the common key, such as a ProductID.

Step 2: Analysis and Visualization

- With this relationship, you can now create visualizations that display sales data by product, category, or any relevant attribute from the Product table.

Best Practices for Model Relationships

Effective management of model relationships is critical for a well-functioning Power BI model. Here are some best practices to consider:

1. Consistent Naming: Use clear and consistent naming conventions for table columns and relationships to enhance understanding.

2. Avoid Circular Relationships: Circular relationships can lead to ambiguity and errors; avoid them whenever possible.

3. Use Bi-Directional Filtering with Caution: Bi-directional filtering can have unintended consequences, so use it thoughtfully and test thoroughly.

4. Implement Security Filters: Utilize role-based security to control access to specific data based on user roles and relationships.

In this section, we will explore the crucial aspect of managing model relationships within Power BI. Properly defining and managing relationships between tables is vital for accurate data analysis and creating meaningful reports.

Illustrative Example: Managing Model Relationships

Scenario:

Imagine you're a retail company with two primary data tables: "Sales" and "Products." You need to create a robust data model that allows you to analyze sales data and product information effectively. Here's a simplified view of your data:

Data Structure:

- Sales Table:

  - Columns: "Date," "ProductID," "Quantity Sold," "Revenue"

- Products Table:

  - Columns: "ProductID," "Product Name," "Category," "Price"

Model Relationships:

1. One-to-Many Relationship: Sales to Products

  - The "Sales" table and the "Products" table are related through the "ProductID" column. This relationship signifies that each sale (row in "Sales") is related to a specific product (row in "Products").

  Relationship Direction:

  - From "Sales" (One) to "Products" (Many)

2. Filter Direction: Both (Both tables filter each other)

Scenario Analysis:

1. Total Revenue by Product Category:

   - You can create a report that displays total revenue by product category using a visual. The relationship between the "Sales" and "Products" tables allows you to aggregate revenue while taking product categories into account.

2. Best-Selling Products:

   - With these relationships, you can identify the best-selling products by analyzing the quantity sold and revenue from the "Sales" table and cross-referencing the product names from the "Products" table.

Benefits:

- Properly managing these model relationships enables you to create informative reports and analyze your data more effectively. You can easily explore insights such as which product categories generate the most revenue, the best-selling products, and their sales trends over time.

Conclusion

Managing model relationships is a fundamental aspect of designing a robust Power BI data model. By understanding the types of relationships, cardinality, and best practices, you can create a data model that provides meaningful insights for your organization.

Part 5. Handling Relationships in Power BI

5.1 One-to-One, One-to-Many, and Many-to-Many Relationships

Effective data modeling in Power BI relies on mastering different types of relationships between tables. In this section, we will explore one-to-one, one-to-many, and many-to-many relationships, providing in-depth insights and practical examples.

Understanding Relationship Types

One-to-One (1:1) Relationship:

A one-to-one relationship implies that one record in a table is related to one and only one record in another table. These relationships are less common but are used when two tables have a shared attribute.

Example:

- Consider a scenario where you have an Employee table and a Manager table. Each employee reports to one and only one manager, creating a one-to-one relationship between the EmployeeID in both tables.

One-to-Many (1:N) Relationship:

A one-to-many relationship is the most common type. It indicates that one record in a table can be related to many records in another table.

Example:

- In the context of a Sales table and a Product table, a one-to-many relationship is established. Each sale is linked to one product, but each product can be associated with many sales, making it a one-to-many relationship.

Many-to-Many (N:M) Relationship:

Many-to-many relationships are used to connect multiple records in one table to multiple records in another table. However, Power BI doesn't support direct N:M relationships, so they are typically implemented using bridge tables.

Example:

- To handle a many-to-many relationship between students and courses, a bridge table is introduced. The bridge table connects students to courses, allowing each student to enroll in multiple courses and each course to have multiple students.

Illustrative Example: One-to-Many Relationship

Let's consider a one-to-many relationship between a Customer table and an Order table:

Step 1: Creating the Relationship

- Establish a one-to-many relationship between the Customer table and the Order table, connecting the CustomerID from both tables.

Step 2: Practical Usage

- With this relationship, you can analyze data such as the total order value for each customer, customer segmentation, and customer order history.

Conclusion

Mastering one-to-one, one-to-many, and many-to-many relationships is crucial for effective data modeling in Power BI. These relationships allow you to structure your data model to provide valuable insights and enable meaningful analysis.

Certainly, here's an illustrative example for the section on "5.1. One-to-One, One-to-Many, and Many-to-Many Relationships" in your book "Power BI: Mastering DAX for Advanced Data Modeling."

Suppose you are building a data model for a retail business that tracks sales and products. Your data model consists of the following tables:

1. Sales Table

  - Contains information about each sale, including a unique SaleID, Date, CustomerID, and ProductID.

2. Customers Table

  - Stores details about customers, including a unique CustomerID, Name, and Contact Information.

3. Products Table

  - Contains information about the products sold, including a unique ProductID, Product Name, Price, and Category.

Types of Relationships:

One-to-One Relationship:

- A one-to-one relationship exists when each record in one table is associated with only one record in another table, and vice versa. In our example, you might establish a one-to-one relationship between the Customers Table and the Sales Table to link each sale to a specific customer.

One-to-Many Relationship:

- A one-to-many relationship exists when each record in one table can be associated with multiple records in another table. In our case, a one-to-many relationship is created between the Products Table and the Sales Table, as one product can appear in multiple sales transactions.

Many-to-Many Relationship:

- A many-to-many relationship is established when multiple records in one table are related to multiple records in another table. This relationship type is often achieved by using a bridge or junction table. For our example, you could have a bridge table to track which products are associated with which sales, allowing multiple products to be associated with multiple sales.

Example Scenario:

Let's consider a specific scenario. A customer named Alice (CustomerID 101) makes a purchase on a specific date. Alice buys two different products: a laptop and a smartphone. Each of these products is associated with a unique ProductID (e.g., Laptop - ProductID 201, Smartphone - ProductID 202).

- Sales Table:

  - SaleID: 1

  - Date: 2023-01-15

  - CustomerID: 101

  - ProductID: 201

- Products Table:

  - ProductID: 201

  - Product Name: Laptop

  - Price: $900

- Products Table:

  - ProductID: 202

  - Product Name: Smartphone

  - Price: $600

Relationships in Action:

- A one-to-one relationship links the SaleID in the Sales Table to the CustomerID in the Customers Table, allowing you to trace the sale back to Alice.

- A one-to-many relationship connects the ProductID in the Sales Table to the ProductID in the Products Table, enabling you to retrieve details about each product sold in that transaction.

- A many-to-many relationship, if applicable, would be established through a bridge table to track the connections between sales and products, allowing you to analyze sales data from various angles.

Understanding these types of relationships is essential for creating efficient and accurate data models in Power BI. It ensures that you can generate valuable insights from your data, whether you're analyzing sales, customer behavior, or any other aspect of your business.

5.2. Cross-Filtering and Context Transition

In the realm of Power BI data modeling, mastering the concepts of cross-filtering and context transition is essential for creating meaningful and interactive reports. This section delves into the intricacies of cross-filtering, context transition, and how to harness their power to build insightful dashboards and reports.

Understanding Cross-Filtering

Cross-filtering, often referred to as "filter propagation," is the mechanism through which filter context flows between related tables in a Power BI model. It's the process by which filtering one table affects the context in another table, allowing for coordinated filtering actions.

Example:

- Consider a scenario where you have a Sales table and a Product table with a one-to-many relationship. When you filter the Product table to select a specific product category, the Sales table automatically updates to display sales data for that chosen category. This is cross-filtering in action.

Context Transition in DAX

Context transition is closely related to cross-filtering and is a fundamental concept in DAX. It refers to how DAX formulas dynamically adapt to the current filter context applied to a table or column. DAX measures and calculations respond to changes in context, ensuring accurate results.

Example:

- If you create a DAX measure to calculate the total sales for a specific product category, the measure will adapt to the filter context applied to the Product table, producing accurate results based on the selected category.

Hierarchies and Drill-Through

Cross-filtering and context transition become particularly powerful when dealing with hierarchies. In Power BI, hierarchies are structures that enable users to drill down into data, focusing on higher or lower levels of detail.

Illustrative Example: Cross-Filtering and Hierarchies

Let's consider a scenario where you have a Date table with a hierarchical structure (Year, Quarter, Month, Day). You want to analyze sales data over time.

Step 1: Hierarchical Filtering

- You create a visual that displays sales over time.

- Initially, the visual shows sales for all years.

Step 2: Drill Down

- Users can drill down into the data by selecting a specific year, quarter, or month within the hierarchy.

- As they make selections, cross-filtering and context transition dynamically adjust the filter context, narrowing the focus to the chosen time period.

In this section, we'll delve into the concept of cross-filtering and context transition in Power BI. To understand this better, let's use an example:

Illustrative Example: Sales and Products Data Model

Imagine you are working with a data model that tracks sales and products. Your data model has the following tables:

1. Sales Table

   - Contains details of each sale, including SaleID, Date, CustomerID, and ProductID.

2. Customers Table

   - Stores customer information, including CustomerID, Name, and Location.

3. Products Table

   - Holds information about the products, including ProductID, Product Name, and Price.

4. Calendar Table

   - A date table that helps you analyze data over time, containing Date, Month, Quarter, and Year.

Scenario: Cross-Filtering and Context Transition

Let's say you want to analyze sales data for a specific year, such as 2023. You want to see the total sales for each product in that year, as well as the top customers who made purchases in that year. In this scenario, cross-filtering and context transition come into play.

1. Filtering by Year:

   - You apply a filter to select the year 2023 in your report. This filter is applied to the Calendar Table.

2. Total Sales by Product:

- You create a visual that shows the total sales by product. In this case, the context transition occurs. The filter on the Calendar Table (2023) flows into the Products Table and Sales Table. Only sales data for 2023 is considered.

3. Top Customers in 2023:

- You also create a visual to display the top customers for the year 2023. Here, context transition is critical. The filter on the Calendar Table (2023) impacts the Customers Table and Sales Table. Only customer data related to sales in 2023 is considered.

Example Data:

Here's a simplified set of data to illustrate the concept:

- Calendar Table:

  - Date: 2023-01-01 to 2023-12-31

- Products Table:

  - ProductID: 201 (Laptop)

  - ProductID: 202 (Smartphone)

- Sales Table:

  - SaleID: 1

  - Date: 2023-03-15

  - CustomerID: 101

  - ProductID: 201

- Customers Table:

 - CustomerID: 101

 - Name: Alice

 - Location: New York

Cross-Filtering and Context Transition in Action:

- You filter for the year 2023.

- The total sales by product visual displays only the sales that occurred in 2023 for products 201 and 202.

- The top customers visual shows only customers like Alice (CustomerID 101) who made purchases in 2023.

Understanding cross-filtering and context transition is vital for accurate data analysis in Power BI. It allows you to focus on the specific data you need, filter information effectively, and derive valuable insights from your datasets, whether you're analyzing sales, customer behavior, or any other data-driven aspect of your business.

Conclusion

Cross-filtering and context transition are essential concepts in Power BI, enabling dynamic and interactive data exploration. Understanding how these mechanisms work and how to use them in your reports empowers you to create engaging and informative dashboards.

5.3. Hierarchies and Parent-Child Relationships

Hierarchies and parent-child relationships play a vital role in structuring and visualizing data effectively in Power BI. In this section, we will explore the concepts of hierarchies and parent-child relationships, their uses, and provide real-world examples to illustrate their value in data modeling.

Understanding Hierarchies

A hierarchy is a structured arrangement of data where individual items are organized into levels of detail. Hierarchies enable users to drill down into data, starting from a high-level summary and progressively moving to more granular information.

Example:

- In a time hierarchy, you may have levels such as Year, Quarter, Month, and Day. Users can start by viewing annual data and then drill down into quarterly, monthly, and daily data.

Creating Hierarchies in Power BI

In Power BI, hierarchies can be established by creating a hierarchy within a table. For example, you can create a Date hierarchy by combining Year, Quarter, Month, and Day attributes.

Illustrative Example: Time Hierarchy

Let's consider a time hierarchy within a Date table:

Step 1: Creating the Hierarchy

- Build a hierarchy in the Date table that combines Year, Quarter, Month, and Day attributes.

Step 2: Visualizing the Hierarchy

- When you use this hierarchy in visuals, such as a line chart, users can start by viewing data at the year level.

Step 3: Drill Down

- Users can interact with the visual to drill down into specific quarters, months, and even days as needed.

Parent-Child Relationships

Parent-child relationships are a specialized type of relationship that links data within a single table. They are typically used for hierarchical data structures where each record relates to a parent record and can have child records.

Example:

- In an organization chart, each employee may have a supervisor (parent) and can have subordinates (children).

Creating Parent-Child Relationships

In Power BI, parent-child relationships are established by defining relationships within a single table, typically using a self-referencing key.

Illustrative Example: Organizational Structure

Consider an example of an organizational structure where each employee record is related to a parent record representing their supervisor:

Step 1: Defining the Relationship

- Establish a parent-child relationship within the Employee table using a self-referencing key like SupervisorID.

Step 2: Visualizing the Structure

- You can create visuals, such as org charts, that utilize the parent-child relationship to display the organization's structure.

In this section, we'll explore the use of hierarchies and parent-child relationships in Power BI. Let's illustrate this with a practical example:

Illustrative Example: Organizational Hierarchy

Imagine you're tasked with analyzing an organizational hierarchy. Your data model includes an "Employees" table, where each employee is linked to their manager through a parent-child relationship. Additionally, the table contains information such as EmployeeID, EmployeeName, Position, and ManagerID.

Scenario: Analyzing Organizational Hierarchy

Suppose you want to create a visual that shows the total number of employees at each level of the organizational hierarchy. This is where hierarchies and parent-child relationships become essential.

Example Data:

Here's a simplified set of data to illustrate the concept:

- Employees Table:
  - EmployeeID: 101
  - EmployeeName: John
  - Position: CEO
  - ManagerID: Null (No manager as John is the CEO)

  - EmployeeID: 201
  - EmployeeName: Sarah
  - Position: VP of Sales
  - ManagerID: 101 (Sarah reports to John)

  - EmployeeID: 202
  - EmployeeName: Mark
  - Position: Sales Manager
  - ManagerID: 201 (Mark reports to Sarah)

  - EmployeeID: 301
  - EmployeeName: Emily
  - Position: Sales Representative
  - ManagerID: 202 (Emily reports to Mark)

Hierarchies and Parent-Child Relationships in Action:

1. Creating a Hierarchy:

   - In Power BI, you can create a hierarchy based on the "EmployeeName" field and "Position" field to visualize the organizational structure.

2. Visualizing Employee Counts:

   - You can create a visual that displays the total number of employees at each level of the hierarchy.

   - This visual allows you to see that there is one CEO (John), one VP of Sales (Sarah), one Sales Manager (Mark), and one Sales Representative (Emily).

Hierarchies and Parent-Child Relationships in Analysis:

- Hierarchies and parent-child relationships enable you to represent complex organizational structures efficiently. You can drill down or expand the hierarchy to explore different levels and get a clear view of how employees are organized within the company.

Understanding the usage of hierarchies and parent-child relationships is crucial for creating insightful visualizations in Power BI, especially when dealing with data that involves hierarchical structures, such as organizational charts.

Conclusion

Hierarchies and parent-child relationships are powerful tools in Power BI for organizing and visualizing hierarchical data. Understanding how to create and utilize hierarchies and parent-child relationships empowers you to provide meaningful insights and interactive reporting.

6.1. Creating and Managing Hierarchies

Hierarchies are a fundamental element in Power BI that allows users to navigate through data in a structured way, providing insights at various levels of granularity. In this section, we will explore the creation and management of hierarchies in Power BI, highlighting their importance in data modeling.

Understanding Hierarchies in Power BI

A hierarchy in Power BI represents a structured arrangement of data attributes, where users can drill down from summarized data to detailed data. Hierarchies make it easier to analyze data, offering a structured path for exploration.

Creating Hierarchies

Creating hierarchies in Power BI involves combining related attributes into a single hierarchy structure. This hierarchy can be built using existing fields or calculated columns.

Example: Time Hierarchy

Let's consider a time hierarchy, which is a common example:

Step 1: Select Attributes

- Choose the time-related attributes, such as Year, Quarter, Month, and Day, that you want to include in your hierarchy.

Step 2: Create Hierarchy

- Combine these selected attributes into a single hierarchy structure within your Date table.

Step 3: Visualization

- Utilize this hierarchy in your visuals, such as line charts, to enable users to drill down from yearly data to quarterly, monthly, and daily data.

Managing Hierarchies

Hierarchies may need adjustments as your reporting needs change or as you identify better ways to organize your data. Managing hierarchies involves tasks like adding or removing attributes and defining the display order of hierarchy levels.

Illustrative Example: Modifying a Product Hierarchy

Consider a scenario where you have a Product hierarchy that includes Category, Subcategory, and Product Name.

Step 1: Modify Hierarchy

- You may decide to add a new attribute, Brand, to the Product hierarchy.

Step 2: Adjust Visuals

- After modifying the hierarchy, update your visuals to include the Brand level, enabling users to explore products by brand.

Best Practices for Hierarchies

Effective hierarchy design is essential for creating user-friendly and insightful reports. Here are some best practices to consider:

1. Keep Hierarchies Concise: Avoid creating overly complex hierarchies with too many levels to prevent overwhelming users.

2. Regularly Review and Adjust: Continuously assess the hierarchy's effectiveness and make adjustments as needed to meet changing reporting requirements.

3. Test User Experience: Test the user experience to ensure that hierarchies are intuitive and easy to navigate.

In this section, we'll delve into the creation and management of hierarchies in Power BI. Let's illustrate this with a practical example:

Illustrative Example: Product Category Hierarchy

Suppose you are working with sales data and need to create a product category hierarchy to analyze sales performance.

Scenario: Product Category Hierarchy

Imagine your data model contains a "Products" table with fields like ProductID, ProductName, Category, and Subcategory. You want to create a hierarchy based on these fields to visualize sales data.

Example Data:

Here's a simplified set of data to illustrate the concept:

- Products Table:
  - ProductID: 1
  - ProductName: Laptop
  - Category: Electronics
  - Subcategory: Computers

  - ProductID: 2
  - ProductName: Smartphone
  - Category: Electronics
  - Subcategory: Mobile Phones

  - ProductID: 3
  - ProductName: Desk
  - Category: Furniture
  - Subcategory: Office Furniture

Creating a Product Category Hierarchy:

1. Create the Hierarchy:

  - In Power BI, you can create a hierarchy by selecting the "Category" and "Subcategory" fields from the "Products" table.

2. Visualizing Sales Data:

   - After creating the hierarchy, you can use it to build visuals that display sales data. For instance, you can create a bar chart that shows total sales by product category and subcategory.

Example Hierarchy Levels:

- Level 1: Category (Electronics, Furniture)

  - Under Electronics:

    - Level 2: Subcategory (Computers, Mobile Phones)

  - Under Furniture:

    - Level 2: Subcategory (Office Furniture)

Hierarchy in Analysis:

- Using hierarchies, you can easily drill down to different levels to analyze sales data. For instance, you can start at the highest level (Category) and then drill down to see sales performance at the Subcategory level.

- This hierarchy simplifies the analysis of complex sales data and enables you to gain insights into which product categories and subcategories are driving sales.

- Managing hierarchies allows you to control the structure and presentation of the data for more intuitive and efficient analysis.

Creating and managing hierarchies in Power BI is a powerful tool for visualizing and exploring data, especially when dealing with multi-level categorization like product categories and subcategories in this example.

Conclusion

Hierarchies are powerful tools in Power BI for organizing and visualizing data. Understanding how to create and manage hierarchies enables you to build informative and interactive reports that provide users with the flexibility to explore data at different levels of granularity.

.

6.2. Role-Playing Dimensions in Multidimensional Models

Role-playing dimensions are a crucial aspect of multidimensional modeling in Power BI. This section explores the concept of role-playing dimensions, their significance, and how to effectively use them to enhance data modeling and reporting.

Understanding Role-Playing Dimensions

In Power BI, role-playing dimensions refer to the practice of using the same dimension table in a model multiple times, each time with a different role. Each role-playing instance of the dimension serves a distinct purpose and allows users to analyze data from different perspectives.

Example: Date Dimension

Consider a Date dimension table used in various ways:

1. As an Order Date: To analyze data by the date when orders were placed.

2. As a Ship Date: To analyze data by the date when orders were shipped.

3. As a Delivery Date: To analyze data by the date when orders were delivered.

Creating Role-Playing Dimensions

Creating role-playing dimensions involves duplicating a dimension table within the Power BI model and assigning unique roles to each instance. These roles define the purpose of each dimension instance.

Illustrative Example: Date Dimension

Let's illustrate the use of a Date dimension with role-playing instances:

Step 1: Duplicate the Date Dimension

- Duplicate the Date dimension table to create instances for Order Date, Ship Date, and Delivery Date.

Step 2: Assign Roles

- Assign distinct roles to each instance, such as 'Order Date,' 'Ship Date,' and 'Delivery Date.'

Step 3: Usage in Reports

- Utilize each instance in reports to analyze data based on the specific date perspective, whether it's order placement, shipping, or delivery.

Benefits of Role-Playing Dimensions

Role-playing dimensions offer several advantages in multidimensional modeling:

1. Enhanced Analysis: They enable users to analyze the same data from various angles, providing more comprehensive insights.

2. User-Friendly Reports: Users can easily switch between different roles in reports, simplifying data exploration.

3. Reduced Model Complexity: Rather than creating multiple similar tables, role-playing dimensions keep the model tidy and efficient.

Best Practices for Role-Playing Dimensions

When working with role-playing dimensions, consider the following best practices:

1. Clear Naming: Ensure that each role-playing instance is named clearly to avoid confusion.

2. Consistent Hierarchies: Maintain consistent hierarchies within role-playing instances to ensure a seamless user experience.

3. Documentation: Document the purpose of each instance and its role to assist other report developers and users.

In this section, we'll explore the concept of role-playing dimensions in multidimensional data models. Role-playing dimensions occur when a single dimension is used in multiple ways within the same model, serving different purposes. Let's illustrate this with a practical example:

Illustrative Example: Date Dimension as a Role-Playing Dimension

Suppose you're building a multidimensional data model to analyze sales data, and you have a date dimension that needs to serve multiple date-related roles:

Scenario: Sales Analysis with Date Roles

You have a Sales data model with a "Date" dimension, and you need to use the same "Date" dimension for various date-related analysis scenarios.

Example Data:

Here's a simplified set of data to illustrate the concept:

- Sales Fact Table:

  - DateKey: A unique identifier for each date

  - SalesAmount: The amount of sales made on that date

Role-Playing Dimensions:

1. Order Date:

   - In one scenario, you want to analyze sales by the order date.

2. Ship Date:

   - In another scenario, you want to analyze sales by the ship date.

3. Due Date:

   - In a third scenario, you want to analyze sales by the due date.

Using the Date Dimension:

- To handle these different date roles, you use the same "Date" dimension but create multiple instances of it, each serving a unique role.

- You set up relationships in the data model to connect the Sales Fact Table with the appropriate date role in the Date Dimension.

Analysis Scenarios:

1. Order Date Analysis:

  - You create a report to analyze sales based on the order date, which tells you when the orders were placed.

2. Ship Date Analysis:

  - In a different report, you analyze sales based on the ship date, which tells you when the orders were actually shipped.

3. Due Date Analysis:

  - Yet another report allows you to analyze sales based on the due date, which is when the payment is due.

Benefits of Role-Playing Dimensions:

- Role-playing dimensions allow you to reuse a single dimension in various ways, simplifying your model and providing flexibility for different analysis scenarios.

- You can create separate reports for each date role without the need to duplicate the Date dimension.

- This approach enables you to gain insights into sales patterns related to order dates, shipping dates, and due dates independently, making your analysis more versatile.

Role-playing dimensions are a valuable technique in multidimensional data modeling, as they streamline the analysis of different aspects of your data using a single shared dimension.

Conclusion

Role-playing dimensions are a valuable tool in Power BI for multidimensional modeling. Understanding how to create and use them effectively allows you to provide users with flexible and insightful reporting options.

6.3. Hierarchical DAX Functions

Hierarchical DAX functions are powerful tools in Power BI for working with data hierarchies and nested structures. In this section, we will explore the concept of hierarchical DAX functions, their significance, and provide practical examples to demonstrate how they can be applied effectively in data modeling.

Understanding Hierarchical DAX Functions

Hierarchical DAX functions are designed to navigate and perform calculations within hierarchies and nested data structures. They are particularly useful when dealing with data that has a parent-child relationship or hierarchical attributes.

Example: Organizational Hierarchy

Consider an organizational hierarchy with employees and their supervisors. Hierarchical DAX functions can help calculate the depth of an employee's position in the hierarchy or retrieve information about their direct reports.

Common Hierarchical DAX Functions

Several DAX functions are tailored for hierarchical data structures. These functions include:

1. PATH: Returns the path of an item in a hierarchy.

2. PATHLENGTH: Calculates the length of the path to an item in a hierarchy.

3. EARLIER: References a previous row in the hierarchy.

4. FILTER: Filters a table based on conditions within the hierarchy.

5. LOOKUPVALUE: Retrieves values based on hierarchical relationships.

Illustrative Example: PATH and PATHLENGTH

Let's illustrate the use of PATH and PATHLENGTH functions in an organizational hierarchy:

Step 1: Create a Hierarchical Table

- Establish a table with hierarchical data, representing an organizational structure.

Step 2: Define the Hierarchy

- Define a hierarchy based on the relationship between employees and their supervisors.

Step 3: Using PATH and PATHLENGTH

- Utilize the PATH function to retrieve the path from an employee to the CEO.

- Use the PATHLENGTH function to calculate the depth of an employee in the hierarchy.

Benefits of Hierarchical DAX Functions

Hierarchical DAX functions offer several benefits for data modeling and analysis:

1. Accurate Calculations: They enable precise calculations within hierarchical structures, providing insights into relationships and positions.

2. Dynamic Reporting: These functions make reports dynamic by allowing users to explore hierarchical data effortlessly.

3. Simplified Formulas: Hierarchical DAX functions simplify complex calculations and reduce the need for extensive formula writing.

Best Practices for Using Hierarchical DAX Functions

When working with hierarchical DAX functions, consider the following best practices:

1. Understand Data Structure: Thoroughly understand the data structure and hierarchy to apply the right functions.

2. Testing: Test hierarchical DAX functions on sample data to ensure accuracy before deploying them in production reports.

3. Documentation: Document the functions and their application to assist other report developers and users.

Certainly, here's an illustrative example for the section on "6.3. Hierarchical DAX Functions" in your book "Power BI: Mastering DAX for Advanced Data Modeling."

In this section, we'll delve into the use of hierarchical DAX functions to work with hierarchical data structures. Let's explore this concept with a practical example:

Illustrative Example: Organizational Hierarchy Analysis

Imagine you're tasked with analyzing the organizational hierarchy of a company. Your data model includes an "Employee" dimension with a hierarchical structure, and you want to use DAX functions to gain insights into this hierarchy.

Example Data:

Here's a simplified set of data to illustrate the concept:

- Employee Dimension Table:

  - EmployeeID: A unique identifier for each employee

  - EmployeeName: The name of the employee

  - ManagerID: The ID of the employee's manager

Hierarchical DAX Functions:

- In this scenario, you can use hierarchical DAX functions to navigate and analyze the organizational structure.

Analysis Scenarios:

1. Employee Reporting Structure:

   - You want to create a report that displays each employee and their immediate manager.

   Hierarchical DAX Function:

   ```DAX
   = PATH("EmployeeHierarchy"[EmployeeID], "EmployeeHierarchy"[ManagerID])
   ```

2. Count of Subordinates:

   - You're interested in finding out how many subordinates each employee has.

   Hierarchical DAX Function:

   ```DAX
   = COUNTROWS(FILTER('EmployeeHierarchy', PATHCONTAINS("EmployeeHierarchy", 'EmployeeHierarchy'[ManagerID], "EmployeeHierarchy"[EmployeeID])))
   ```

3. Managerial Depth:

   - You'd like to determine the depth of the managerial hierarchy for each employee.

Hierarchical DAX Function:

```DAX
= MAXX(FILTER('EmployeeHierarchy', 'EmployeeHierarchy'[EmployeeID] = 'EmployeeHierarchy'[ManagerID]), PATHLENGTH("EmployeeHierarchy"[EmployeeID]))
```

Benefits of Hierarchical DAX Functions:

- Hierarchical DAX functions enable you to explore and analyze hierarchical data structures in your organization efficiently.

- You can create reports and measures that provide valuable insights, such as reporting structures, subordinate counts, and managerial depths, which are essential for HR and management decision-making.

- These functions simplify the process of traversing hierarchies and extracting relevant information for a deeper understanding of the organizational structure.

By leveraging hierarchical DAX functions, you can gain valuable insights into the hierarchical relationships within your organization, providing data-driven decision support for management and HR departments.

Conclusion

Hierarchical DAX functions are indispensable in Power BI for analyzing data with hierarchical attributes and parent-child relationships. Understanding how to leverage these functions empowers you to create more insightful reports and perform complex calculations within hierarchies.

CHAPTER III
Advanced DAX Techniques

Part 7. Time Intelligence Functions in DAX

7.1. Mastering Time Intelligence Patterns

Time intelligence is a crucial aspect of data modeling in Power BI, enabling users to analyze data across different time periods and make meaningful comparisons. In this section, we will explore the concept of time intelligence patterns, their significance, and provide practical examples to demonstrate how they can be applied effectively in data modeling.

Understanding Time Intelligence Patterns

Time intelligence patterns are established techniques for performing calculations on time-based data, such as sales data over months or years. These patterns provide a structured approach to address common time-related questions, such as year-to-date (YTD) calculations, moving averages, and period-over-period comparisons.

Common Time Intelligence Patterns

Several time intelligence patterns are widely used in Power BI. These patterns include:

1. YTD (Year-to-Date): Calculating values from the beginning of the year up to the current date.

2. QTD (Quarter-to-Date): Summarizing values from the start of the quarter to the current date.

3. MTD (Month-to-Date): Aggregating data from the beginning of the month to the current date.

4. Moving Averages: Calculating the average of values over a moving window of time.

5. Period-over-Period Comparisons: Comparing data between different time periods.

Illustrative Example: Year-to-Date (YTD) Calculation

Let's illustrate the use of the YTD time intelligence pattern:

Step 1: Define the Measure

- Create a DAX measure that calculates the YTD total sales.

Step 2: Filter Data

- Apply a filter to consider only the data from the beginning of the year up to the current date.

Step 3: Visualization

- Use this YTD measure in your visuals to display year-to-date sales data.

Benefits of Time Intelligence Patterns

Time intelligence patterns offer several benefits for data modeling and analysis:

1. Consistency: They provide a consistent and reliable approach to time-related calculations.

2. Efficiency: Using predefined patterns saves time and effort compared to building custom calculations.

3. Comparability: Time intelligence patterns allow for easy comparisons between different time periods.

Best Practices for Using Time Intelligence Patterns

When working with time intelligence patterns, consider the following best practices:

1. Clear Naming: Name your time intelligence measures and columns in a way that clearly indicates their purpose, making it easier for users to identify them.

2. Documentation: Document the use of time intelligence patterns and the logic behind them to assist other report developers and users.

In this section, we'll explore how to master time intelligence patterns in DAX to analyze and compare data across different time periods. Let's consider an example related to sales data for a retail company:

Illustrative Example: Sales Analysis Using Time Intelligence

Scenario:

Imagine you are the data analyst for a retail company, and you want to perform a sales analysis to gain insights into the company's performance over different time periods. You have a sales dataset with the following fields:

- Sales Date: The date when the sale occurred.

- Product: The product sold.

- Quantity Sold: The quantity of each product sold.

- Revenue: The revenue generated from each sale.

Time Intelligence Patterns:

We'll use DAX time intelligence patterns to analyze this data:

1. Total Sales Over Time:

   - You want to calculate the total sales over a specific time frame, such as a month or a quarter.

   Time Intelligence DAX Pattern:

```DAX
Total Sales = SUM('Sales'[Revenue])
```

2. Year-over-Year Growth:

   - You're interested in calculating the year-over-year (YoY) growth in sales revenue.

   Time Intelligence DAX Pattern:

```DAX
YoY Growth = DIVIDE([Total Sales], CALCULATE([Total Sales],
DATEADD('Calendar'[Date], -1, YEAR)))
```

3. Moving Average:

   - You want to create a moving average of monthly sales to smooth out fluctuations and identify trends.

   Time Intelligence DAX Pattern:

```DAX
3-Month Moving Average = AVERAGEX(
    FILTER('Calendar', AND('Calendar'[Date] <= MAX('Calendar'[Date]), 'Calendar'[Date] >= MAX('Calendar'[Date]) - 90)),
    [Total Sales]
)
```

Analysis Results:

By applying these time intelligence patterns, you can:

- Calculate total sales for specific time periods, helping you understand the company's overall performance.

- Determine the YoY growth to identify trends and fluctuations in sales.

- Create moving averages to identify longer-term trends and make informed business decisions.

Using these time intelligence patterns, you can gain valuable insights into your sales data and make data-driven decisions to improve business performance and strategy.

Conclusion

Mastering time intelligence patterns is essential for creating insightful reports and performing meaningful analysis in Power BI. Understanding how to apply these patterns empowers you to answer common time-related questions and gain deeper insights into your data.

7.2. Custom Time-Intelligence Calculations

While standard time intelligence patterns are essential, there are situations in which you may need to create custom time-intelligence calculations to address specific business requirements. In this section, we will explore the concept of custom time-intelligence calculations, their significance, and provide practical examples to demonstrate how to design and implement them effectively in data modeling.

Understanding Custom Time-Intelligence Calculations

Custom time-intelligence calculations refer to bespoke DAX measures that are tailored to meet unique business needs related to time-based data. These calculations are created when standard time-intelligence patterns are insufficient, and they often involve combining DAX functions and operators in novel ways.

Common Scenarios for Custom Time-Intelligence Calculations

Custom time-intelligence calculations may be needed in various scenarios, such as:

1. Non-standard Fiscal Calendars: When a fiscal year doesn't align with a typical calendar year.

2. Special Date Handling: Addressing specific holidays, seasonality, or unusual business events.

3. Dynamic Comparisons: Performing complex period-over-period comparisons that cannot be achieved with standard patterns.

4. Custom Moving Averages: Calculating unique moving averages or trends based on business-specific requirements.

Illustrative Example: Custom Fiscal Year Calculation

Let's illustrate the creation of a custom fiscal year calculation:

Step 1: Define the Measure

- Create a DAX measure that calculates sales based on a custom fiscal year definition.

Step 2: Date Mapping

- Map your custom fiscal year to the standard calendar year by specifying the starting month and any year offsets.

Step 3: Visualization

- Use this custom measure in your visuals to display sales data according to the custom fiscal year.

Benefits of Custom Time-Intelligence Calculations

Custom time-intelligence calculations offer several benefits for data modeling and analysis:

1. Flexibility: They provide flexibility in addressing unique business requirements that cannot be met with standard patterns.

2. Tailored Insights: Custom calculations yield insights that are directly relevant to your specific business context.

3. Competitive Advantage: Creating custom time-intelligence solutions can give your organization a competitive edge in data analysis.

Best Practices for Creating Custom Time-Intelligence Calculations

When designing custom time-intelligence calculations, consider the following best practices:

1. Clear Documentation: Document the logic and purpose of your custom calculations to ensure they are understood by other team members and report developers.

2. Testing and Validation: Thoroughly test your custom calculations on a range of scenarios to ensure their accuracy and reliability.

In this section, we'll delve into creating custom time-intelligence calculations in DAX to address specific business needs. Let's consider an example of a retail company that wants to analyze its sales data using custom time-intelligence calculations:

Illustrative Example: Custom Time-Intelligence Calculations

Scenario:

You are working with a retail company that wants to perform an in-depth analysis of their sales data. They want to create custom time-intelligence calculations to gain insights into sales trends and seasonality.

Sales Data:

The dataset includes the following fields:

- Sales Date: The date when a sale occurred.

- Product: The product sold.

- Quantity Sold: The quantity of each product sold.

- Revenue: The revenue generated from each sale.

Custom Time-Intelligence Calculations:

1. Sales Growth Over Previous Year:

   - The company wants to calculate the sales growth compared to the same period in the previous year.

   Custom Time-Intelligence DAX Calculation:

```DAX
Sales Growth YoY = DIVIDE([Total Sales] - [Total Sales Last Year], [Total Sales Last Year])
```

2. Seasonal Decomposition:

- They want to decompose sales data into trend, seasonality, and residual components using a custom algorithm.

Custom Time-Intelligence DAX Calculation:

Custom algorithm or formula to decompose the time series data into trend, seasonality, and residual components.

Analysis Results:

With these custom time-intelligence calculations, the retail company can:

- Gain a deeper understanding of sales growth over the previous year, helping them assess performance.

- Decompose the sales data to identify patterns and seasonality, which can aid in inventory planning and marketing strategies.

By tailoring time-intelligence calculations to their specific needs, the company can make more informed decisions and optimize their business operations based on the insights derived from their sales data.

Conclusion

Custom time-intelligence calculations are indispensable for addressing unique time-related challenges in data modeling. Understanding how to create and apply these custom calculations empowers you to tailor your reports to the specific needs of your business and gain deeper insights into your data.

7.3. Comparing Periods and Rolling Averages

Comparing periods and calculating rolling averages are essential techniques in data modeling that enable users to gain insights into data trends and variations over time. In this section, we will explore the concept of comparing periods and calculating rolling averages in DAX, their significance, and provide practical examples to demonstrate how to use these techniques effectively in data analysis.

Understanding Comparing Periods

Comparing periods involves assessing the performance or values of one period against another. This technique allows users to make comparisons between, for example, this month and the previous month, or this quarter and the same quarter in the previous year.

Illustrative Example: Monthly Sales Comparison

Let's consider an example of comparing monthly sales:

Step 1: Define the Measure

- Create a DAX measure that calculates monthly sales.

Step 2: Lag Function

- Use DAX functions like LAG to calculate the sales of the previous month.

Step 3: Visualization

- Present the data by comparing current month sales with the previous month's sales in your visuals.

Understanding Rolling Averages

Rolling averages, also known as moving averages, are used to smooth out data trends by calculating the average of data points within a specific window of time. This technique is helpful for identifying long-term patterns and trends in data, eliminating short-term fluctuations.

Illustrative Example: Three-Month Rolling Average

Let's illustrate the calculation of a three-month rolling average:

Step 1: Define the Measure

- Create a DAX measure that calculates the rolling average of sales over a three-month period.

Step 2: AVERAGEX Function

- Use the AVERAGEX function to calculate the average of the sales data within a rolling three-month window.

Step 3: Visualization

- Present the data by showing the three-month rolling average in your visuals.

Benefits of Comparing Periods and Rolling Averages

Comparing periods and calculating rolling averages offer several benefits for data analysis and reporting:

1. Identifying Trends: These techniques help in identifying trends and patterns in data, allowing for informed decision-making.

2. Smoothing Data: Rolling averages help in smoothing out data to focus on long-term trends and eliminate short-term noise.

3. Comparative Analysis: Comparing periods enables comparisons between different time frames, helping users evaluate performance changes.

Best Practices for Comparing Periods and Calculating Rolling Averages

When using these techniques, consider the following best practices:

1. Data Cleansing: Ensure data quality and consistency before applying these techniques to avoid distortions.

2. Visualization: Use appropriate visualizations to effectively convey comparisons and rolling averages.

In this section, we'll explore how to use DAX to compare different periods and calculate rolling averages. Let's consider an example of a company that wants to analyze their monthly website traffic data:

Illustrative Example: Comparing Periods and Rolling Averages

Scenario:

You are working with a company that wants to evaluate its website traffic data and understand how it's changing over time. They want to compare monthly website traffic and calculate rolling averages to identify trends.

Website Traffic Data:

The dataset includes the following fields:

- Date: The date for each data point.

- Visits: The number of website visits on that date.

DAX Calculations:

1. Month-over-Month Comparison:

  - The company wants to compare the number of visits for each month to the previous month.

  Custom DAX Calculation:

```DAX
MoM Change = [Visits] - CALCULATE([Visits], DATEADD('Table'[Date], -1, MONTH))
```

2. Quarterly Rolling Average:

  - They want to calculate a rolling average of website visits for each quarter, using the past 3 months' data.

Custom DAX Calculation:

```DAX
3-Month Rolling Avg = AVERAGEX(
    FILTER('Table', 'Table'[Date] >= EARLIER('Table'[Date]) - 90 && 'Table'[Date] <= EARLIER('Table'[Date])),
    [Visits]
)
```

Analysis Results:

By applying these custom DAX calculations to their website traffic data, the company can:

- Evaluate month-over-month changes to identify which months experienced significant increases or decreases in website visits.

- Calculate a quarterly rolling average to understand longer-term trends and fluctuations in website traffic.

This analysis enables the company to make data-driven decisions for marketing campaigns, content strategy, and resource allocation to optimize their online presence and engagement.

Conclusion

Comparing periods and calculating rolling averages are invaluable techniques in data analysis, providing insights into trends and variations over time. Understanding how to apply these techniques empowers you to gain a deeper understanding of your data and make data-driven decisions.

Part 8. Handling Errors and Exception Scenarios

8.1. Error Handling Techniques in DAX

Error handling is a crucial aspect of data modeling and DAX formula creation. In this section, we will delve into the concept of error handling techniques in DAX, their significance, and provide practical examples to demonstrate how to manage errors effectively in your data models.

Understanding Error Handling in DAX

DAX formulas can generate errors for various reasons, such as dividing by zero, referencing missing values, or encountering circular dependencies. Error handling techniques are essential for ensuring that your data models remain robust and provide meaningful insights.

Common Error Types in DAX

Before we dive into error handling techniques, it's important to understand the common error types in DAX:

1. #DIV/0! Error: This error occurs when dividing by zero or an empty result.

2. #VALUE! Error: This error arises when the data type is not appropriate for the operation.

3. #BLANK Error: This error indicates a missing or null value.

Illustrative Example: Handling Division by Zero

Let's consider an example of handling division by zero:

Step 1: Identify the Error Scenario

- Recognize that a DAX formula division operation may result in a #DIV/0! error.

Step 2: Implement Error Handling

- Use DAX error handling functions like DIVIDE to handle division by zero gracefully.

Step 3: Visualization

- Present the data with appropriate error handling in your visuals, ensuring that no #DIV/0! errors are displayed.

Error Handling Functions in DAX

DAX provides various functions to manage errors, such as:

1. IFERROR: This function returns an alternate value when an error occurs.

2. DIVIDE: DIVIDE handles division errors gracefully and allows you to specify a replacement value.

3. ISBLANK: ISBLANK checks for blank values and helps you avoid erroneous calculations.

Benefits of Error Handling in DAX

Effective error handling offers several advantages for data modeling and analysis:

1. Robust Models: Error handling ensures that your data models can handle unexpected situations without breaking.

2. Data Quality: It helps maintain data quality by managing missing or erroneous data gracefully.

3. Enhanced User Experience: Error-free visuals and reports provide a better experience for users.

Best Practices for Error Handling in DAX

When implementing error handling in DAX, consider the following best practices:

1. Clear Error Messages: Provide meaningful error messages to aid in troubleshooting.

2. Testing and Validation: Test error handling techniques thoroughly to ensure they function as expected.

In this section, we'll explore error handling techniques in DAX. Let's consider an example where you're working with financial data, and you want to handle scenarios where data might be missing or contain errors:

Illustrative Example: Error Handling Techniques in DAX

Scenario:

You are an analyst working with financial data, and you need to calculate the average quarterly revenue for a company. However, the data may contain missing values or anomalies that could affect the accuracy of your analysis.

Financial Data:

The dataset includes the following fields:

- Quarter: The financial quarter (Q1, Q2, Q3, Q4).

- Revenue: The quarterly revenue of the company.

DAX Calculations:

1. Handling Missing Values:

   - You want to calculate the average quarterly revenue while accounting for missing values.

   Custom DAX Calculation:

```DAX
Average Quarterly Revenue = DIVIDE(
    SUM('Table'[Revenue]),
    COUNTROWS(FILTER('Table', NOT(ISBLANK('Table'[Revenue]))))
)
```

2. Handling Anomalies:

- You suspect there might be anomalies in the data that could significantly impact the average. You want to exclude any quarterly revenue figures that deviate too far from the mean.

Custom DAX Calculation:

```DAX
Filtered Average Revenue = AVERAGEX(

    FILTER('Table', 'Table'[Revenue] >= (AVERAGE('Table'[Revenue]) * 0.5) && 'Table'[Revenue] <= (AVERAGE('Table'[Revenue]) * 1.5)),

    'Table'[Revenue]

)
```

Analysis Results:

By using these error handling techniques in DAX, you can:

- Calculate the average quarterly revenue while handling missing values gracefully.

- Exclude quarterly revenue figures that deviate significantly from the mean, reducing the impact of anomalies on your analysis.

These techniques ensure that your financial analysis is more robust and provides more accurate insights, even in the presence of missing data or anomalies in the dataset.

Conclusion

Error handling is an essential skill in DAX data modeling, ensuring the integrity and reliability of your data models. Understanding how to manage errors effectively empowers you to create robust models that deliver accurate and meaningful insights.

8.2. Dealing with Missing Data

In the world of data analysis and modeling, missing data is a common challenge that every professional must navigate. Whether it's gaps in your data source, unexpected null values, or unavailability of information for certain periods, dealing with missing data is essential for accurate analysis and visualization in Power BI. In this section, we will explore techniques and strategies to effectively handle missing data using Data Analysis Expressions (DAX).

Understanding the Impact of Missing Data:

Missing data can have significant consequences for your analyses. Inaccurate calculations, skewed visualizations, and incomplete insights can result from ignoring or mishandling missing data. Before delving into the solutions, it's important to understand the potential consequences of missing data in your Power BI reports and dashboards.

Identifying Missing Data:

The first step in addressing missing data is to identify where and why it occurs in your dataset. We'll walk you through methods for spotting gaps and null values, and provide guidance on data profiling techniques that can help you determine the scope and impact of the missing data.

Strategies for Handling Missing Data:

1. Data Imputation: We'll explore methods for imputing missing data points, including using statistical measures, interpolation, and domain-specific knowledge.

2. Handling Null Values: Learn how to use DAX functions to handle null values effectively. We'll cover functions like `IFNULL`, `COALESCE`, and more to transform or replace null values as needed.

3. Advanced Filtering: Discover techniques for creating dynamic filters and measures that adapt to the presence of missing data, ensuring your visualizations remain accurate.

Illustrative Examples:

Throughout this section, we'll provide real-world examples and scenarios to illustrate the strategies in action. You'll see how to use DAX functions and calculated columns to address specific issues related to missing data, and how these solutions impact your Power BI reports.

This section provides detailed insights into dealing with missing data, along with real-world examples. Feel free to make any adjustments or provide additional information if needed.

In this section, we will explore how to handle missing data effectively using DAX. Let's consider an example where you are working with a sales dataset, and you need to calculate the total sales for each product category, but the dataset contains missing values.

Illustrative Example: Dealing with Missing Data

Scenario:

You are a data analyst working with a sales dataset, and you want to calculate the total sales for each product category. However, the dataset may contain missing values for some products, and you need to handle these missing values gracefully.

Sales Data:

The dataset includes the following fields:

- Product Category: The category of the product (e.g., Electronics, Clothing, Furniture).
- Sales Amount: The sales amount for each product.

DAX Calculations:

1. Handling Missing Values:

   - You want to calculate the total sales for each product category while handling missing values.

   Custom DAX Calculation:

   ```DAX
   Total Sales by Category = SUMX(
       SUMMARIZE(FILTER('Table', NOT(ISBLANK('Table'[Sales Amount]))), 'Table'[Product Category], 'Table'[Sales Amount]),
       [Sales Amount]
   )
   ```

Analysis Results:

By using this DAX calculation, you can:

- Calculate the total sales for each product category while gracefully handling missing values. The `FILTER` function filters out rows with missing sales values before summarizing the data.

This technique ensures that you get accurate insights into the total sales for each product category, even when dealing with missing data in the dataset.

8.3. Addressing Circular Dependencies

Circular dependencies can pose significant challenges in data modeling, leading to unexpected results and errors in DAX formulas. In this section, we will explore the concept of circular dependencies, their impact on data models, and effective strategies to address them.

Understanding Circular Dependencies

Circular dependencies occur when the relationships between tables in a data model form a closed loop. In such cases, it becomes challenging to determine the correct order of evaluation for DAX formulas, potentially leading to incorrect results and performance issues.

Detecting Circular Dependencies

Before addressing circular dependencies, it's crucial to detect them. Power BI provides tools and methods for identifying circular dependencies within your data model.

Illustrative Example: Detecting Circular Dependencies

Let's consider an example to understand how circular dependencies can be detected:

Step 1: Use Power BI's Built-in Tools

- Power BI offers built-in features to help you identify circular dependencies. These tools can highlight relationships that form a closed loop.

Step 2: Visual Representation

- Visualize the relationships between tables in your data model to identify loops or cycles.

Strategies for Addressing Circular Dependencies

Once circular dependencies are detected, it's essential to address them effectively to maintain data model integrity. The following strategies can be employed:

1. Reevaluate Table Structure: Review the table structure and relationships to determine if any tables can be merged or redesigned to eliminate circular dependencies.

2. Use Bridge Tables: Introduce bridge tables or junction tables to break the circular relationship and create a one-to-many relationship, resolving the circular dependency.

3. Modify DAX Formulas: Adjust DAX formulas to minimize the impact of circular dependencies by changing the evaluation context.

Illustrative Example: Using Bridge Tables

Suppose you have circular dependencies in your data model due to relationships between Table A and Table B, and Table B and Table C. You can introduce a bridge table (Table D) to resolve the issue:

- Table D establishes relationships with Table A and Table C, breaking the circular dependency.

Benefits of Resolving Circular Dependencies

Effective resolution of circular dependencies provides several advantages:

1. Correct Results: Eliminating circular dependencies ensures that DAX formulas generate accurate results.

2. Enhanced Performance: Addressing circular dependencies can lead to improved query and calculation performance.

3. Maintaining Data Model Integrity: Resolving circular dependencies maintains the integrity and reliability of your data model.

Best Practices for Circular Dependency Resolution

When addressing circular dependencies, consider the following best practices:

1. Document Changes: Maintain clear documentation of the changes made to resolve circular dependencies for future reference.

2. Testing: Thoroughly test the data model to ensure that the changes have resolved the issue without introducing new errors.

In this section, we will explore how to deal with circular dependencies in your data modeling using DAX. Circular dependencies can occur when you have tables that reference each other, creating a loop that can affect calculations. Let's consider a scenario and how to address it.

Illustrative Example: Addressing Circular Dependencies

Scenario:

You are working with a budgeting and actuals dataset in Power BI. You have two tables: "Budget" and "Actuals." The "Budget" table contains budget figures for various cost centers, and the "Actuals" table contains actual spending data for those cost centers. You want to calculate the variance between the budgeted and actual spending while avoiding circular dependencies.

Data Structure:

- Budget Table:

  - Columns: "Cost Center," "Budget Amount"

- Actuals Table:

  - Columns: "Cost Center," "Actual Amount"

DAX Calculations:

1. Calculating Variance:

  - You want to create a DAX measure to calculate the variance between the budgeted and actual spending without encountering circular dependencies.

Custom DAX Calculation:

```DAX
Variance = SUM('Budget'[Budget Amount]) - SUM('Actuals'[Actual Amount])
```

Addressing Circular Dependencies:

- By creating a separate measure for the variance, you avoid circular dependencies between the "Budget" and "Actuals" tables.

- This allows you to calculate the variance in your reports without encountering issues related to circular dependencies.

This approach ensures that you can effectively calculate variances between budgeted and actual spending while maintaining a clean and efficient data model without circular dependencies.

Conclusion

Addressing circular dependencies is a critical aspect of advanced data modeling in Power BI. This section equips readers with the knowledge and strategies needed to detect, resolve, and prevent circular dependencies effectively. Through illustrative examples and best practices, readers will gain the expertise to ensure the accuracy and reliability of their data models.

.

Part 9. Advanced DAX Patterns and Best Practices

9.1. Data Modeling Patterns

Effective data modeling is the cornerstone of successful Power BI solutions. Data modeling patterns are essential frameworks that help you structure your data for insightful analysis and report creation. In this section, we will explore various data modeling patterns and their significance in Power BI.

Understanding Data Modeling Patterns

Data modeling patterns are predefined structures that simplify how data tables are organized in your Power BI model. These patterns are particularly useful when dealing with complex data sources, multiple relationships, and large datasets. They ensure that your model is efficient, scalable, and capable of delivering meaningful insights.

Common Data Modeling Patterns:

1. Star Schema:

  - The Star Schema is a widely used pattern where you have a central fact table containing measures and dimension tables that provide context. This pattern simplifies data relationships and enhances query performance.

  Example: In a retail model, the "Sales" table serves as the fact table, while "Products," "Customers," and "Time" act as dimension tables.

2. Snowflake Schema:

- The Snowflake Schema is an extension of the Star Schema where dimension tables are normalized into sub-dimensions. It reduces data redundancy but may slightly impact query performance.

Example: In a healthcare model, the "Patients" dimension may be further normalized into "Demographics" and "Medical History" sub-dimensions.

3. Date Table Patterns:

- Creating a separate date table with various time-related attributes is a common pattern to support time intelligence calculations.

Example: A date table might include attributes like "Date," "Month," "Quarter," and "Year."

Benefits of Data Modeling Patterns:

- Improved Query Performance: Patterns like the Star Schema enhance query performance by simplifying relationships and aggregations.

- Scalability: Using patterns allows your model to scale effectively as your data grows.

- Maintainability: Patterns make your model more understandable and maintainable, especially for complex datasets.

Illustrative Example: Star Schema

Scenario:

Imagine you're building a Power BI model for an e-commerce platform. You have two primary data tables: "Sales" and "Products," among others.

Data Structure:

- Sales Table:

  - Columns: "OrderDate," "ProductID," "Quantity Sold," "Revenue"

- Products Table:

  - Columns: "ProductID," "Product Name," "Category," "Price"

Model Structure:

In this scenario, you can use the Star Schema pattern to structure your model. The "Sales" table serves as the central fact table containing measures, while the "Products" table acts as a dimension table providing context.

Benefits:

This Star Schema pattern simplifies data relationships, improves query performance, and allows you to create meaningful reports and analyses, such as total revenue by product category or sales trends over time.

Conclusion:

Data modeling patterns are fundamental in Power BI. They provide structure and organization to your data, allowing for efficient, scalable, and insightful reporting. Whether you choose a Star Schema, Snowflake Schema, or date table pattern, selecting the right pattern for your specific use case is key to mastering data modeling in Power BI.

9.2. Query Optimization Techniques

Effective query optimization is crucial for ensuring your Power BI reports and dashboards run efficiently, especially when working with large datasets. This section explores various query optimization techniques and strategies that will help you enhance the performance of your Power BI solutions.

Understanding Query Optimization in Power BI

Query optimization in Power BI focuses on improving the speed and efficiency of data retrieval and calculations. When you build complex reports with numerous visuals, it's vital to ensure your queries are as fast as possible to deliver a smooth user experience.

Common Query Optimization Techniques:

1. Import Mode vs. DirectQuery Mode:

  - One of the first decisions to make is whether to use the Import mode or DirectQuery mode. In Import mode, data is loaded into Power BI, which can enhance performance for smaller datasets. In DirectQuery mode, data stays in the source database, providing real-time access but potentially impacting performance.

2. Data Modeling Simplification:

- Ensure your data model is well-structured, uses appropriate relationships, and leverages data modeling patterns (as discussed in the previous section). A clean and efficient data model will significantly impact query performance.

3. Calculated Columns vs. Measures:

- Understanding when to use calculated columns and measures is essential. Calculated columns are computed during data loading, which can impact import performance. Measures are calculated on the fly and generally provide faster query performance.

Optimization Strategy:

Scenario:

Imagine you're working with a large dataset containing customer data, sales transactions, and product information. Users have reported that report loading times are slower than desired.

Query Optimization Techniques Applied:

1. Import vs. DirectQuery:

- In this scenario, you've determined that most users don't need real-time access to the data. You've opted to switch from DirectQuery mode to Import mode to speed up query performance.

2. Data Modeling Refinement:

- You've reviewed your data model, ensured it follows the appropriate data modeling patterns (as discussed in section 9.1), and eliminated unnecessary relationships that were slowing down queries.

3. Measures Usage:

- You've replaced certain calculated columns with measures, particularly for calculations that are only needed in specific visuals. This shift to measures reduces data model complexity and results in faster query performance.

Benefits:

By implementing these query optimization techniques, you've significantly improved report loading times, making the user experience more efficient and enjoyable.

Conclusion:

Query optimization is a crucial aspect of Power BI development, especially when working with substantial datasets. The selection of the appropriate mode (Import or DirectQuery), a well-structured data model, and the strategic use of measures all contribute to faster query performance, ensuring that your Power BI reports and dashboards run smoothly and provide users with actionable insights.

9.3. Real-World DAX Best Practices

Real-world scenarios often present unique challenges in Power BI development. To ensure success, it's essential to follow best practices that are not only specific but also practical and adaptable to a wide range of situations. In this section, we'll explore real-world DAX best practices and provide examples that demonstrate their application.

Best Practices in Real-World DAX Development:

1. Parameterized DAX Measures:

- Consider a scenario where you need to create measures that dynamically adapt to user-selected criteria. Parameterized DAX measures allow users to choose specific dimensions, filters, or time frames. For example, a user might want to see sales figures for different product categories and time periods. Creating parameterized DAX measures facilitates this flexibility.

- Example:

Let's say you have a DAX measure for calculating total sales, but you want to allow users to select a specific category to focus on. By parameterizing your DAX measure, users can dynamically change the category for analysis.

2. DAX Error Handling:

- Real-world data is often messy and may contain missing or erroneous data. Implementing robust error handling in your DAX measures is crucial. This includes dealing with errors, such as divide by zero, or handling missing values gracefully.

- Example:

Consider a scenario where you're calculating a profit margin using DAX, and some of your cost values are missing or zero. Robust error handling in your DAX measures can prevent calculation errors and return meaningful results.

3. Performance Optimization:

- In real-world scenarios with large datasets, query and report performance can become a significant concern. Applying DAX best practices to optimize performance involves techniques such as query folding, avoiding redundant calculations, and optimizing relationships.

- Example:

Imagine a scenario where your report loads slowly due to a complex DAX measure. By optimizing the measure, you can significantly improve the report's load time.

Benefits of Real-World DAX Best Practices:

Implementing these real-world DAX best practices can yield several benefits:

- Enhanced Flexibility: Parameterized DAX measures provide users with the ability to explore data from different angles and criteria.

- Data Integrity: Effective error handling ensures that your DAX calculations produce accurate results, even with imperfect data.

- Improved Performance: Performance optimization techniques result in faster report load times and a more responsive user experience.

Conclusion:

Real-world DAX development requires practical and adaptable best practices that address the specific challenges and opportunities presented by your data and user needs. By incorporating parameterization, error handling, and performance optimization into your DAX development, you can create Power BI solutions that not only meet your users' needs but also perform efficiently and accurately in diverse scenarios. These real-world DAX best practices empower you to deliver actionable insights in a dynamic and ever-changing data environment.

CHAPTER IV
DAX for Specific Use Cases

Part 10. Financial Analysis and Forecasting with DAX

10.1. Implementing Financial KPIs

Financial analysis and forecasting are critical components of business intelligence. Key Performance Indicators (KPIs) provide valuable insights into an organization's financial health and performance. In this section, we will explore how to implement financial KPIs using DAX in Power BI. We will cover various financial metrics and provide practical examples to illustrate their application.

Financial KPIs in Power BI:

1. Revenue Metrics:

  - Gross Revenue: Gross revenue represents the total income generated before deducting any costs or expenses. It's a fundamental KPI that reflects the overall sales or revenue of a business.

  - Net Revenue: Net revenue deducts expenses such as returns and allowances from gross revenue, providing a more accurate picture of income.

  - Revenue Growth: This KPI measures the percentage change in revenue over a specific period, indicating the trend in sales performance.

- Revenue Per Customer: It calculates the average revenue generated per customer and is valuable for understanding customer profitability.

2. Profitability Metrics:

- Gross Profit Margin: The gross profit margin is the percentage of revenue left after deducting the cost of goods sold (COGS). It measures the efficiency of a company's production and pricing.

- Net Profit Margin: Net profit margin is the percentage of revenue remaining after all expenses, including COGS, operating expenses, and taxes, have been deducted.

- Return on Investment (ROI): ROI measures the profitability of an investment relative to its cost, often used for evaluating the success of projects or marketing campaigns.

3. Liquidity Metrics:

- Current Ratio: The current ratio measures a company's ability to cover its short-term liabilities with short-term assets. It's crucial for assessing liquidity and financial stability.

- Quick Ratio: The quick ratio is a more stringent liquidity measure, excluding inventory from current assets. It provides a clearer picture of a company's ability to pay its short-term debts.

Example Application:

Let's consider a practical example of implementing financial KPIs in Power BI. Imagine you are working with a retail company's sales data. To calculate the "Gross Profit Margin," you would use DAX to subtract the cost of goods sold (COGS) from gross revenue and divide the result by gross revenue. This DAX measure will provide a dynamic view of the gross profit margin, allowing you to track and analyze profitability over time.

```DAX
Gross Profit Margin = DIVIDE([Gross Revenue] - [COGS], [Gross Revenue])
```

By creating DAX measures for each financial KPI, you can build a comprehensive financial dashboard that provides real-time insights into your organization's financial performance.

Conclusion:

Implementing financial KPIs using DAX in Power BI empowers organizations to make data-driven decisions and gain a deeper understanding of their financial health and performance. These KPIs, such as revenue metrics, profitability metrics, and liquidity metrics, provide actionable insights that drive financial analysis and forecasting. By leveraging DAX, you can build dynamic and interactive reports that enable users to explore and interpret financial data effectively.

10.2. Forecasting Models and Techniques

Forecasting is an essential aspect of business analysis, enabling organizations to make informed decisions and plan for the future. In this section, we will explore how to implement forecasting models and techniques using DAX in Power BI. We will delve into various methods and practical examples to illustrate their application.

Forecasting Methods in Power BI:

1. Moving Averages:

- Simple Moving Average (SMA): SMA calculates the average of a specified number of data points over a defined period. It is useful for smoothing out fluctuations in data and identifying trends.

- Exponential Moving Average (EMA): EMA gives more weight to recent data points, making it responsive to recent changes. It is suitable for capturing short-term trends.

2. Time Series Decomposition:

- Trend Analysis: Identifying and modeling the long-term trend in data, which helps in understanding overall growth or decline.

- Seasonal Decomposition: Isolating seasonal patterns within data to account for recurring patterns that impact business operations.

3. Regression Analysis:

- Linear Regression: Utilizing DAX to build linear regression models to predict future values based on historical data.

- Nonlinear Regression: Employing DAX for nonlinear regression models, suitable when data relationships are not linear.

Example Application:

Let's consider a practical example of implementing forecasting models in Power BI. Suppose you are working with a retail company's sales data and want to forecast future sales. You can use

DAX to calculate a simple moving average (SMA) to smooth out sales data and identify trends. The formula for calculating a 5-period SMA for sales might look like this:

```DAX
5-Period SMA = AVERAGE(Sales[Total Sales], -5, 0)
```

The negative and zero values in the AVERAGE function represent the current and past periods, respectively, for calculating the moving average. By visualizing this SMA in Power BI, you can provide stakeholders with insights into sales trends and forecasts for the upcoming periods.

Conclusion:

Implementing forecasting models and techniques using DAX in Power BI equips organizations with the tools to anticipate future trends and make data-driven decisions. Whether you choose moving averages, time series decomposition, or regression analysis, DAX empowers you to analyze historical data and generate valuable forecasts. These forecasts, along with visualizations in Power BI, enable stakeholders to gain insights into future business performance and strategically plan for what lies ahead.

10.3. Budgeting and Scenario Analysis

Budgeting and scenario analysis are vital components of financial planning and analysis. In this section, we will explore how to implement budgeting and scenario analysis using DAX in Power BI. We will delve into various methods and practical examples to illustrate their application.

Budgeting in Power BI:

Budgeting in Power BI involves creating models that allow organizations to set financial goals and monitor their progress. DAX provides various functions and techniques to facilitate this process.

1. Setting Budget Assumptions:

   - Defining key budget assumptions such as revenue growth, cost projections, and expense allocations.

2. Creating Budget Measures:

   - Using DAX to create budget measures that capture the budgeted values for various financial KPIs.

3. Budget Variance Analysis:

   - Calculating variances between budgeted and actual values to assess financial performance against budget assumptions.

Scenario Analysis:

Scenario analysis in Power BI enables organizations to evaluate different financial scenarios, make informed decisions, and plan for various business outcomes.

1. Creating Multiple Scenarios:

- Using DAX to set up multiple scenarios with different assumptions, such as optimistic, pessimistic, and baseline scenarios.

2. Scenario Measures:

   - Calculating scenario-specific measures to assess the impact of different assumptions on financial KPIs.

3. Visualization of Scenarios:

   - Visualizing scenarios in Power BI reports to provide stakeholders with insights into potential outcomes.

Example Application:

Let's consider a practical example of budgeting and scenario analysis in Power BI. Suppose you are working with a manufacturing company, and you want to set up a budget for the next fiscal year. You can use DAX to create budget measures for revenue, expenses, and profit based on predefined assumptions. Additionally, you can create scenario-specific measures for optimistic, pessimistic, and baseline scenarios to analyze the impact on profitability.

For instance, the formula for calculating budgeted profit might look like this:

```DAX
Budgeted Profit = [Budgeted Revenue] - [Budgeted Expenses]
```

To perform scenario analysis, you can adjust key assumptions for each scenario and see the resulting impact on financial measures. Visualizations in Power BI can help stakeholders understand how different scenarios may affect the company's financial health.

Conclusion:

Implementing budgeting and scenario analysis in Power BI with DAX empowers organizations to set financial goals, monitor performance, and make informed decisions. By creating budget measures, performing variance analysis, and conducting scenario analysis, businesses can gain valuable insights into their financial future. These insights enable stakeholders to make strategic decisions, adapt to changing circumstances, and plan for various financial scenarios, ultimately enhancing financial stability and success.

11.1. Sales Funnel Analysis

Sales funnel analysis is a critical aspect of sales and marketing analytics in Power BI. In this section, we will explore how to leverage DAX to perform sales funnel analysis, which is essential for understanding the customer journey, optimizing sales processes, and maximizing revenue.

Understanding the Sales Funnel:

A sales funnel represents the various stages that a potential customer goes through before making a purchase. These stages typically include:

1. Awareness: The customer becomes aware of a product or service.

2. Interest: The customer shows interest in the offering.

3. Consideration: The customer considers purchasing.

4. Intent: The customer expresses intent to buy.

5. Evaluation: The customer evaluates different options.

6. Purchase: The customer makes a purchase.

Sales Funnel Analysis with DAX:

Sales funnel analysis in Power BI involves the use of DAX to:

1. Track Conversion Rates:

- Create DAX measures to track the conversion rates from one stage to the next. For example, the conversion rate from "Awareness" to "Interest."

2. Visualize Funnel Progress:

   - Use visualizations in Power BI to display the progression of customers through each stage of the funnel. Visuals like funnel charts and bar charts are commonly used.

3. Identify Bottlenecks:

   - Utilize DAX measures to identify bottlenecks or drop-offs in the funnel, indicating where potential customers are being lost in the process.

Example Application:

Let's consider a real-world example. You work for an e-commerce company and want to analyze the sales funnel for an online product. Using DAX in Power BI, you can create measures to track the conversion rates between stages, such as "Awareness" to "Interest" and "Interest" to "Consideration."

For instance, the formula for calculating the conversion rate from "Awareness" to "Interest" might look like this:

```DAX
Conversion Rate (Awareness to Interest) = DIVIDE([Number of Customers in Interest Stage], [Number of Customers in Awareness Stage])
```

By visualizing this data, you can see where potential customers drop off in the funnel, allowing you to make informed decisions about improving the sales process.

Conclusion:

Sales funnel analysis using DAX in Power BI is a powerful tool for businesses to track and optimize their sales and marketing efforts. It helps identify areas for improvement, measure the effectiveness of different marketing campaigns, and enhance overall sales strategies. By applying DAX to analyze the sales funnel, organizations can gain a competitive edge and maximize their revenue potential.

11.2. Marketing Campaign Performance

Marketing campaign performance analysis using DAX in Power BI is instrumental in evaluating the effectiveness of marketing strategies, measuring the return on investment (ROI), and making data-driven decisions for future campaigns. In this section, we will delve into specific DAX techniques and concepts for analyzing marketing campaigns.

Key Metrics and Measures:

Before we dive into the technical aspects, let's understand the key metrics and measures that are commonly used in marketing campaign analysis:

1. Click-Through Rate (CTR): CTR measures the effectiveness of an online advertising campaign. It is calculated as the ratio of clicks to impressions.

2. Conversion Rate: Conversion rate is the percentage of users who take a desired action after interacting with an ad. Actions can include making a purchase, signing up for a newsletter, or downloading an e-book.

3. Return on Investment (ROI): ROI quantifies the profitability of a marketing campaign by comparing the gains (returns) to the costs.

4. Customer Acquisition Cost (CAC): CAC represents the cost of acquiring a new customer, which is calculated by dividing the total campaign cost by the number of new customers acquired.

DAX Techniques for Marketing Campaign Analysis:

1. Calculating CTR and Conversion Rate:

To calculate CTR and conversion rate, you can create DAX measures in Power BI. For example, to calculate CTR:

```DAX
CTR = DIVIDE([Clicks], [Impressions])
```

Similarly, to calculate the conversion rate:

```DAX
Conversion Rate = DIVIDE([Conversions], [Clicks])
```

2. Evaluating ROI:

Calculating ROI is crucial for assessing campaign profitability. DAX can help in comparing campaign costs with the revenue generated. For instance:

```DAX
ROI = DIVIDE([Total Revenue] - [Campaign Cost], [Campaign Cost])
```

3. Customer Segmentation:

Utilize DAX for customer segmentation, which involves categorizing customers based on their behavior, such as high-value customers, repeat buyers, or one-time purchasers. You can employ DAX functions like RANKX and FILTER for this purpose.

Real-World Example:

Imagine you're a marketing manager for an e-commerce company. You recently ran a digital advertising campaign to promote a new product line. By applying DAX in Power BI, you can create a dashboard that provides insights into CTR, conversion rates, ROI, and customer segmentation. You can also compare campaign performance across different channels and demographics.

Conclusion:

Marketing campaign performance analysis with DAX in Power BI is indispensable for optimizing marketing strategies, understanding customer behavior, and maximizing ROI. By employing DAX measures and functions, you can gain actionable insights to refine your marketing efforts, allocate resources effectively, and drive business growth. With these techniques, marketers can make data-driven decisions and ensure that every marketing dollar is well spent.

11.3. Customer Segmentation and Retention

In the realm of sales and marketing analytics, customer segmentation and retention are paramount for businesses striving to enhance their competitiveness, build customer loyalty, and increase revenue. DAX (Data Analysis Expressions) plays a pivotal role in this domain, enabling data professionals to gain insights into customer behavior, segment customers effectively, and implement strategies for customer retention.

Key Concepts and Objectives:

Customer segmentation aims to divide a customer base into distinct groups or segments based on shared characteristics or behaviors. These segments can be defined in various ways, including demographics, psychographics, purchase history, or engagement levels. The ultimate goal is to personalize marketing efforts, tailor product recommendations, and improve customer experience. Segmentation can lead to higher customer satisfaction, conversion rates, and customer retention.

Using DAX for Customer Segmentation:

DAX offers a rich set of functions and measures for effective customer segmentation:

1. RFM Analysis: Recency, Frequency, and Monetary (RFM) analysis is a classic customer segmentation method. DAX measures can help calculate the recency of purchases, the frequency of customer interactions, and the monetary value of transactions. For instance:

```DAX
```

Recency = DATEDIFF(MAX('Sales'[PurchaseDate]), TODAY(), DAY)
```

2. Segmentation by Behavior: Employ DAX to segment customers based on their behavior, such as browsing history, products viewed, or interactions with promotions. For example:

```DAX

Frequent Visitors = CALCULATE(SUM('WebsiteData'[Visits]), FILTER('WebsiteData', 'WebsiteData'[PageViews] > 10))
```

Customer Retention Analysis:

In addition to segmentation, DAX can facilitate customer retention analysis. Understanding customer churn rates and implementing strategies to retain customers is vital for sustained business growth. You can use DAX to calculate churn rates, customer lifetime value (CLV), and identify factors contributing to customer attrition.

Real-World Example:

Consider you are the head of marketing for an e-commerce platform. By utilizing DAX in Power BI, you can segment customers into different categories like frequent shoppers, occasional buyers, or new customers. You can analyze the retention rate of each segment over time and design targeted marketing campaigns to retain and upsell customers.

Conclusion:
```

Customer segmentation and retention analysis are integral components of sales and marketing analytics. DAX empowers data professionals to create effective segments, analyze customer behavior, and develop customer-centric strategies for long-term success. By leveraging DAX measures and functions, organizations can foster customer loyalty, reduce churn, and increase customer lifetime value, ultimately driving business growth and profitability.

Part 12. DAX for HR and Workforce Analytics

12.1. HR Metrics and Key Measures

In the realm of Human Resources (HR) and workforce analytics, understanding and analyzing HR metrics are essential for organizations to manage their employees effectively, make data-driven decisions, and optimize workforce performance. DAX (Data Analysis Expressions) serves as a valuable tool for HR professionals to create meaningful HR metrics and key measures that drive business growth.

Key Concepts and Objectives:

HR metrics are quantifiable measures used to assess various aspects of an organization's workforce. These metrics help HR departments evaluate performance, make informed decisions, and align HR strategies with broader business goals. Key measures in HR encompass areas such as employee productivity, retention, recruitment, training, and diversity.

Using DAX for HR Metrics:

DAX empowers HR professionals to create HR metrics and key measures that provide actionable insights. Here are some HR metrics and how they can be implemented using DAX:

1. Employee Turnover Rate: Calculating the percentage of employees who leave the organization over a specific period. DAX formula:

```DAX
Turnover Rate = DIVIDE(COUNTROWS('HRData'[Employees Left]),
COUNTROWS('HRData'[Total Employees]))
```

2. Employee Productivity: Measuring the productivity of employees based on key performance indicators (KPIs). DAX can be used to calculate KPIs and visualize trends over time.

3. Training Effectiveness: Assessing the effectiveness of training programs by analyzing performance improvements before and after training sessions. DAX can be employed to calculate training ROI and performance changes.

Real-World Example:

Imagine you are an HR manager in a large corporation. By using DAX in Power BI, you can create HR dashboards that track metrics like employee turnover, performance by department, training effectiveness, and diversity ratios. You can visualize these metrics and trends, enabling you to make data-driven decisions on employee retention strategies, training investments, and workforce planning.

Conclusion:

HR metrics and key measures are essential for managing and optimizing an organization's workforce. DAX, with its capabilities in data analysis and visualization, empowers HR professionals to create meaningful HR metrics, track key measures, and make data-driven decisions that lead to a more efficient and productive workforce. By utilizing DAX in HR analytics, organizations can align HR strategies with business objectives and create a more engaged and high-performing workforce, ultimately contributing to business success.

12.2. Workforce Planning and Analytics

Workforce planning and analytics are crucial components of Human Resources (HR) management that focus on strategically aligning an organization's workforce with its business goals. DAX (Data Analysis Expressions) provides powerful tools to analyze workforce data, gain insights, and make data-driven decisions to optimize workforce planning.

Key Concepts and Objectives:

Workforce planning involves forecasting and managing an organization's workforce needs to meet its strategic objectives. DAX can be instrumental in achieving these objectives:

1. Demand Forecasting: Predicting future workforce requirements based on business projections. DAX can analyze historical data to determine hiring needs and trends.

2. Skills Gap Analysis: Identifying gaps in the skills and competencies of the current workforce compared to the skills required for future roles. DAX can evaluate the skillset of employees and pinpoint areas that need development.

3. Retention Analysis: Examining factors that contribute to employee retention or attrition. DAX can be used to calculate metrics like turnover rates and identify patterns that may lead to workforce changes.

Using DAX for Workforce Planning:

DAX can be employed to create dynamic dashboards and reports that facilitate workforce planning:

1. Scenario Analysis: DAX can model various workforce scenarios, such as changes in headcount, employee demographics, and skill development, allowing HR professionals to explore different planning options.

2. Predictive Analytics: Leveraging historical data, DAX can create predictive models that forecast future workforce needs. For instance, you can predict hiring needs based on anticipated sales growth.

Real-World Example:

Consider an HR manager tasked with workforce planning at a technology company. By using DAX in Power BI, they can analyze historical data on employee turnover, skill development, and demand forecasting. They can create interactive dashboards that visualize scenarios like hiring additional software developers to meet project deadlines. This data-driven approach enables better decision-making in workforce planning.

Conclusion:

Workforce planning and analytics are essential for organizations to align their workforce with their business goals. DAX, with its data modeling and analytical capabilities, empowers HR professionals to make strategic decisions based on accurate data. By utilizing DAX for workforce planning and analytics, organizations can ensure they have the right talent with the right skills at the right time, contributing to long-term success and competitiveness in the market.

12.3. Employee Performance and Compensation

Effective management of employee performance and compensation is pivotal for organizations aiming to attract, retain, and motivate their workforce. DAX (Data Analysis Expressions) equips HR professionals with robust tools to analyze and optimize employee performance and compensation strategies.

Key Concepts and Objectives:

Managing employee performance and compensation involves several key components, and DAX can play a crucial role in achieving the following objectives:

1. Performance Metrics: Utilize DAX to create performance metrics, such as Key Performance Indicators (KPIs) and performance scores, based on various data sources, including sales figures, project completion rates, and customer satisfaction scores.

2. Compensation Analysis: Leverage DAX for analyzing and modeling compensation data. Calculate salary adjustments, bonuses, or incentives based on performance metrics, company goals, or market benchmarks.

3. Incentive Programs: Use DAX to design incentive programs that reward high-performing employees, thus fostering motivation and engagement. DAX can help create models that simulate different incentive scenarios and their impact on overall performance.

Using DAX for Employee Performance and Compensation:

DAX is a versatile tool that can be applied to various aspects of employee performance and compensation management:

1. Performance Dashboards: Create dynamic dashboards in Power BI that provide real-time insights into employee performance. Visualizations can include performance trends, achievements, and areas that require improvement.

2. Compensation Modeling: Utilize DAX to model compensation scenarios. For example, you can simulate the impact of different bonus structures on employee motivation and retention.

Real-World Example:

Imagine an HR manager in a manufacturing company who wants to improve employee performance and compensation strategies. Using DAX in Power BI, they can analyze data on production output, quality, and attendance. DAX can help calculate individual performance scores and suggest compensation adjustments based on these scores. Visualizations can provide insights into the effectiveness of these strategies.

Conclusion:

Effective management of employee performance and compensation is vital for any organization. DAX offers a powerful solution for HR professionals to harness data-driven insights and make informed decisions. By leveraging DAX in employee performance and compensation analysis, organizations can improve motivation, retention, and overall performance, which can contribute to long-term success and a competitive edge in the job market.

CHAPTER V
Advanced Visualization Techniques

Part 13. Custom Visualizations with DAX

13.1. Building Custom Charts and Visuals

Power BI provides a wide array of pre-built visualizations, but there are times when you need to create custom charts and visuals to convey data insights that can't be achieved with standard visuals. In this section, we will explore how to use DAX (Data Analysis Expressions) to build custom charts and visuals in Power BI.

Why Create Custom Visuals with DAX:

1. Unique Data Representation: There are instances where your data doesn't fit neatly into standard charts. Creating custom visuals allows you to represent your data in a unique and meaningful way.

2. Visual Storytelling: Custom visuals enable you to craft a visual narrative tailored to your specific audience, which can make your data-driven story more compelling and easier to understand.

3. Interactive Dashboards: Custom visuals can enhance interactivity within your reports. You can design visuals that respond dynamically to user selections and filters, creating a more engaging user experience.

Key Steps in Building Custom Visuals:

Creating custom visuals in Power BI involves several key steps, and DAX plays a pivotal role in this process:

1. Data Preparation: Utilize DAX to transform and prepare your data for custom visuals. This may include aggregations, filtering, and the creation of calculated columns or tables.

2. Visual Design: Use Power BI's native capabilities to design and place custom visuals in your reports. You can build visuals using the DAX formula language in conjunction with custom visuals libraries like D3.js or Plotly.

3. Interaction: Implement DAX measures and calculations that allow users to interact with your custom visuals. For instance, you can create custom slicers or filters that impact the behavior of your visuals based on user selections.

Real-World Example:

Imagine you work for a retail company and you want to create a custom visual that shows the relationship between product sales and weather conditions. Using DAX, you can calculate the correlation between sales and temperature, and then create a custom scatterplot that visualizes this relationship. Furthermore, you can add a slider that allows users to adjust the correlation threshold for specific product categories.

Conclusion:

Building custom charts and visuals using DAX in Power BI is a valuable skill that empowers you to present data in a way that is tailored to your specific requirements. Whether it's representing complex data relationships, crafting interactive dashboards, or telling a unique visual story, DAX-driven custom visuals provide a powerful means to convey insights and engage your audience more effectively. This chapter will explore various DAX techniques and practical examples for building custom visuals in Power BI.

13.2. Interactive and Dynamic Visualizations

In Power BI, interactive and dynamic visualizations are instrumental in transforming data into actionable insights. In this section, we will delve into how to leverage DAX (Data Analysis Expressions) to create interactive and dynamic visualizations, which play a pivotal role in enhancing user engagement and understanding of data.

The Power of Interactive Visualizations:

Interactive and dynamic visualizations allow users to interact with data on a more granular level. These visuals enable users to explore data, change perspectives, and gain insights through their interactions. Here are some key elements that define the power of interactive visualizations:

1. User-Driven Exploration: Interactive visuals empower users to filter, drill down, and slice data based on their preferences. Users can explore data in a way that suits their specific needs.

2. Real-Time Feedback: Dynamic visuals provide real-time feedback as users make selections or changes in the visual. This immediate feedback loop aids in decision-making and understanding.

3. Storytelling: Interactive visuals are excellent tools for data storytelling. You can guide users through the data narrative by allowing them to interact with visuals and uncover insights step by step.

Building Interactive and Dynamic Visualizations with DAX:

Here's a breakdown of the key steps to create interactive and dynamic visualizations using DAX in Power BI:

1. Data Preparation: Utilize DAX to prepare data by creating measures, calculated columns, and tables. Ensure that your data model is well-structured and optimized for interactivity.

2. Selection Logic: Implement DAX measures and calculations that drive interactivity. For instance, you can create dynamic measures that change based on user selections, or use DAX functions like SWITCH to control the display of different data views.

3. Visual Components: Use Power BI's native visualizations and DAX calculations to build interactive components like slicers, filters, and drill-throughs. Also, consider custom visuals for advanced interaction.

Real-World Example:

Suppose you're analyzing a sales dataset, and you want to build an interactive visual that allows users to drill down into sales performance by region, product category, and time period. You can use DAX measures to calculate aggregated values based on user selections in slicers, enabling dynamic visual updates as users explore different aspects of the data.

Conclusion:

Interactive and dynamic visualizations created using DAX in Power BI offer an engaging way to convey insights and encourage user exploration. These visuals are essential in transforming raw data into a powerful tool for data-driven decision-making. In this chapter, we will explore various DAX techniques and practical examples to build interactive and dynamic visualizations that empower users to interact with data effectively, uncover valuable insights, and make informed decisions.

13.3. Advanced DAX for Custom Reports

In this section, we will explore advanced DAX techniques that enable the creation of custom reports with a high degree of flexibility, tailored to the specific needs of users or organizations. Custom reports often require complex calculations and dynamic elements, and DAX is the perfect tool for delivering these requirements.

Understanding the Need for Custom Reports:

Custom reports offer several advantages, such as the ability to:

1. Adapt to Unique Requirements: Custom reports can be tailored to the unique analytical needs of different business units or departments within an organization.

2. Incorporate Complex Calculations: DAX's flexibility allows you to create custom calculations and key performance indicators (KPIs) that may not be possible with standard visualizations.

3. Dynamic Elements: Custom reports can include dynamic elements like advanced filters, conditional formatting, and user interaction, providing a more tailored and interactive experience.

Building Advanced DAX for Custom Reports:

Here are the key steps to building custom reports with advanced DAX:

1. Data Modeling: Start with a well-structured data model that captures all relevant data. Ensure the model is optimized for performance.

2. Measure Development: Create custom DAX measures to calculate the specific KPIs required for the custom report. These measures can range from profitability ratios to advanced forecasting models.

3. Dynamic Filters: Use DAX to create advanced filter logic. For example, you can develop measures that enable conditional filtering based on user input.

4. Conditional Formatting: Implement DAX-based conditional formatting to highlight data points based on predefined criteria or user selections.

5. Parameterization: Develop parameters in DAX that allow users to customize report elements, such as date ranges or scenarios.

6. Custom Visuals: Consider leveraging custom visuals in Power BI to create unique and tailored visualizations that cannot be achieved with standard visuals.

Real-World Example:

Imagine you're working on a custom financial reporting solution. In this scenario, you could use advanced DAX calculations to build custom profitability measures, dynamic filters for slicing data by product or time frame, and sophisticated conditional formatting to highlight areas of interest in the financial reports.

Conclusion:

Advanced DAX techniques are essential for developing custom reports in Power BI that cater to the specific analytical needs of users and organizations. By harnessing the power of DAX, you can create reports that incorporate complex calculations, dynamic elements, and tailored visualizations. These custom reports provide a higher level of flexibility, interactivity, and insight, making them valuable assets for data-driven decision-making.

In the next chapter, we will explore how to leverage custom visuals and advanced DAX techniques to enhance the visualization capabilities of Power BI for specialized reporting requirements.

Part 14. Creating Advanced Dashboards with DAX

14.1. Dashboard Design Principles

Dashboards serve as a crucial tool for data communication and decision-making in modern business intelligence. An effective dashboard not only presents data but also conveys insights, trends, and actionable information to users. In this section, we will explore the key design principles for creating compelling and functional dashboards using DAX in Power BI.

1. Clarity and Simplicity:

An essential design principle is to keep your dashboard clear and simple. Avoid clutter and unnecessary details. Users should quickly grasp the main message and data points without feeling overwhelmed.

Example: Imagine you're designing a sales performance dashboard. Instead of presenting every sales metric at once, focus on the most critical KPIs, such as revenue, sales growth, and top products. Avoid excessive visual elements that distract from the main insights.

2. Visual Hierarchy:

Establish a visual hierarchy that guides users' attention. Key information should be easily noticeable, often through visual cues like color, size, or position. Use formatting to emphasize the most critical data.

Example: In a financial dashboard, highlight significant changes in revenue by using color to distinguish between positive and negative trends. Larger, bold fonts can draw attention to the most important numbers, like quarterly revenue.

3. Consistency:

Maintain consistency in layout, fonts, colors, and terminology across your dashboard. Consistency helps users navigate and understand the data more efficiently.

Example: If you use a specific color scheme for categories in one part of the dashboard, maintain the same colors for similar categories in other sections. This ensures a cohesive visual experience.

4. Contextualization:

Provide context for the data by adding titles, labels, and explanations. Users should understand the significance of the information presented and its relevance to decision-making.

Example: If you're displaying regional sales data, include a clear title and labels to indicate the time frame and the regions represented. Add a brief description to explain the purpose of the dashboard.

5. User-Driven Interactivity:

Enhance your dashboard's usability by incorporating interactive elements. Filters, slicers, and drill-through options allow users to explore the data based on their interests and requirements.

Example: In a supply chain dashboard, allow users to filter data by specific product categories, regions, or time periods. This flexibility enables users to focus on what matters most to them.

6. Responsiveness:

Design dashboards that are responsive to various screen sizes and devices. Ensuring that your dashboard works well on both desktop and mobile devices is crucial for a broader audience.

Example: Test your dashboard's responsiveness by viewing it on different devices, making adjustments as needed to maintain its functionality and readability.

7. Performance Optimization:

Optimize dashboard performance by considering the data model, DAX calculations, and visuals. Ensure that your dashboard loads and responds quickly, even with large datasets.

Example: Use DAX best practices to write efficient calculations and minimize the use of unnecessary visuals and complex measures that might slow down the dashboard.

Conclusion:

Designing effective dashboards in Power BI with DAX is a combination of art and science. By adhering to these design principles, you can create dashboards that are both visually appealing and highly informative. Remember that user feedback and iterative improvements are key to creating dashboards that meet the evolving needs of your audience.

In the next section, we will delve into user-driven interactivity and explore how DAX can be used to create dynamic and responsive dashboards.

14.2. User-Driven Interactivity

User-driven interactivity is a critical aspect of creating compelling and user-friendly dashboards in Power BI. It allows users to explore and analyze data according to their specific needs and preferences. In this section, we will dive into the principles of user-driven interactivity and how to implement it effectively using DAX in Power BI.

1. Filters and Slicers:

Filters and slicers are essential tools for enabling user-driven interactivity. They allow users to focus on specific subsets of data by selecting criteria such as time periods, product categories, or regions.

Example: In a sales dashboard, provide slicers that enable users to choose a particular time frame (e.g., a specific month or year) and filter data accordingly. This empowers users to investigate sales performance for their chosen period.

2. Drill-Through Functionality:

Drill-through functionality enables users to explore data hierarchies or details. It allows users to navigate from summary-level information to more detailed insights.

Example: In a hierarchical data model, like an organizational structure, users can drill through from the executive level to department-level details. This provides context and a deeper understanding of data.

3. Interactive Charts and Visuals:

Utilize interactive chart elements, such as tooltips, to provide additional information when users hover over data points. This enhances the user's ability to gain insights interactively.

Example: In a bar chart displaying product sales, tooltips can show specific sales figures when users hover over individual bars. Users can easily compare values for different products.

4. Cross-Filtering and Highlighting:

Leverage cross-filtering to create connections between visuals. When a user interacts with one visual, it can dynamically affect other visuals on the same page, highlighting relevant information.

Example: If users click on a specific region on a map visual, it can cross-filter a bar chart to display sales data only for that region. This contextual highlighting streamlines data exploration.

5. Bookmarking and Storytelling:

Bookmarking allows you to capture a particular view of the data and save it as a bookmark. You can then create a sequence of bookmarks to tell a data-driven story.

Example: When analyzing yearly sales performance, use bookmarks to create a storytelling experience. Each bookmark represents a different year, allowing users to step through sales data chronologically.

6. Custom Interactivity Using DAX:

DAX calculations can be employed to enable custom interactivity based on specific business needs. You can create measures and calculations that respond to user selections dynamically.

Example: Calculate year-over-year growth as a DAX measure and display it in a card visual. When users select a different year from the slicer, the growth percentage updates accordingly.

7. Mobile Optimization:

Ensure that user-driven interactivity functions smoothly on mobile devices. Design your dashboard with responsive visuals and user interfaces to cater to a broader audience.

Example: When developing a mobile-optimized version of your dashboard, prioritize touch-friendly buttons and controls for seamless interaction.

Conclusion:

User-driven interactivity is an integral part of creating engaging and insightful dashboards. By implementing filters, slicers, drill-through, interactive visuals, and DAX-driven custom interactivity, you empower users to explore data and derive meaningful insights. Keep in mind that the goal is to make data exploration intuitive and customizable, meeting the unique requirements of your audience.

In the next section, we will explore how to embed Power BI dashboards in web applications, extending the reach of your data-driven insights to a wider audience.

14.3. Embedding Dashboards in Web Applications

Embedding Power BI dashboards in web applications is a powerful way to share your data visualizations and insights with a broader audience. It allows you to seamlessly integrate your Power BI reports into your own web applications, portals, or websites, providing a unified experience for your users. In this section, we will explore the process of embedding Power BI dashboards into web applications, highlighting key considerations and providing practical examples.

Understanding Power BI Embedded:

Power BI Embedded is a service provided by Microsoft that enables developers to integrate Power BI content into custom applications. It's designed for scenarios where you want to embed reports and dashboards without requiring users to have Power BI licenses.

Embedding Process Overview:

1. Register Your Application: To embed Power BI dashboards in a web application, you need to register your application in the Azure portal. This registration provides the necessary access and permissions.

2. Authentication: Implement authentication mechanisms in your web application, which can include Azure AD, service principal, or user authentication, depending on your requirements.

3. Embedding the Dashboard: Use Power BI Embedded APIs to programmatically embed the dashboard in your web application. You can specify filters, hide elements, and define interactions as needed.

Example Scenario: Embedding Sales Dashboard

Let's consider a scenario where you want to embed a sales dashboard created in Power BI into your organization's intranet portal.

1. Register Your Application:

- In the Azure portal, create a new App Registration to represent your web application.

- Configure API permissions to allow your app to access Power BI resources.

- Note the Application (client) ID and client secret for authentication.

2. Authentication:

- Implement Azure AD authentication in your web application. Users logging in should have the necessary permissions to view the embedded dashboard.

3. Embedding the Dashboard:

- In your web application code, use the Power BI JavaScript library and REST API to embed the sales dashboard.

- Specify authentication details using the client ID and secret.

- Define filters to show specific data segments. For example, filter the dashboard to show sales data for a particular region.

```javascript
// Sample code to embed Power BI dashboard
const embedConfig = {
  type: 'dashboard',
  id: 'your-dashboard-id',
  embedUrl: 'https://app.powerbi.com/dashboardEmbed?dashboardId=your-dashboard-id',
  tokenType: models.TokenType.Aad,
  accessToken: 'your-access-token',
  settings: {
    filterPaneEnabled: false,
    navContentPaneEnabled: true,
```

```
    },
};


const dashboardContainer = $('#dashboard-container')[0];

const dashboard = powerbi.embed(dashboardContainer, embedConfig);

```
```

4. User Experience:

When users access your web application, they can seamlessly interact with the embedded Power BI dashboard. They can view sales data, apply filters, drill into details, and gain insights without leaving the portal.

Conclusion:

Embedding Power BI dashboards in web applications enhances the reach of your data visualizations and ensures a unified experience for your users. Whether it's sharing sales reports, financial analyses, or HR metrics, the process involves registering your application, setting up authentication, and embedding the dashboard using Power BI Embedded APIs. This integration enables your organization to provide data-driven insights in a seamless manner, extending the power of Power BI beyond the traditional viewer.

In the next section, we will explore best practices and advanced techniques for creating custom visualizations and reports with DAX, further enhancing your data storytelling capabilities.
```

CHAPTER VI
Performance Optimization

Part 15. Performance Tuning and Optimization in DAX

15.1. Identifying Performance Bottlenecks

Optimizing the performance of your Power BI data models is essential to ensure that your reports and dashboards deliver a responsive and efficient user experience. In this section, we will focus on identifying performance bottlenecks within your data models, highlighting key considerations and providing practical examples to help you diagnose and address these issues effectively.

Understanding Performance Bottlenecks:

Performance bottlenecks are specific areas within your Power BI data model where operations slow down, impacting the overall responsiveness of your reports. Identifying these bottlenecks is the first step in the optimization process.

Common Performance Bottlenecks:

1. Large Data Tables: Tables with a high number of rows can lead to slower query response times. These tables often contain transactional data or detailed records.

2. Complex DAX Formulas: Overly complex DAX measures and calculated columns can slow down data retrieval and calculations.

3. Inefficient Relationships: Poorly designed relationships between tables can lead to performance issues, such as unnecessary cross-filtering.

4. Redundant Calculations: Repeated calculations for the same result can consume resources and affect performance.

Diagnosing Performance Bottlenecks:

To identify performance bottlenecks in your Power BI data models, consider the following diagnostic steps:

1. Use Performance Analyzer:

Power BI includes a Performance Analyzer tool that allows you to trace the performance of queries, visuals, and DAX calculations. Use it to identify specific areas with slow response times.

2. Monitor Query Execution:

Monitor query execution times to determine if any specific queries are taking longer than expected. You can use Query Diagnostics in Power BI Service or external profiling tools.

3. Examine Resource Usage:

Analyze the resource usage in the Power BI Service, such as memory and CPU, during report rendering. This can help pinpoint resource-intensive operations.

4. Profile DAX Formulas:

Profile your DAX formulas to identify which measures or calculated columns are consuming the most processing time.

Addressing Performance Bottlenecks:

Once you've identified performance bottlenecks, you can take specific actions to address them:

1. Data Modeling Optimization:

- Simplify large tables: Consider aggregating data when possible to reduce the number of rows.

- Optimize table structure: Review your table relationships and eliminate unnecessary ones.

- Avoid redundant calculations: Ensure that you're not calculating the same values multiple times.

2. DAX Formula Optimization:

- Review complex DAX measures: Simplify DAX expressions and remove unnecessary calculations.

- Use SUMMARIZE: Replace FILTER with SUMMARIZE whenever possible for more efficient filtering.

- Minimize the use of iterators: Iterators like SUMX and AVERAGEX can be resource-intensive.

3. Performance Testing:

Periodically test your reports and dashboards with a substantial dataset to assess their performance under real-world conditions.

Example Scenario: Large Fact Table

In a sales analysis report, you identify a large fact table containing millions of rows, which leads to slow query response times. To address this bottleneck, you decide to aggregate the data at a higher level, such as monthly sales, to improve query performance.

Conclusion:

Identifying and addressing performance bottlenecks is crucial for delivering high-performance Power BI reports and dashboards. By using diagnostic tools, monitoring query execution, examining resource usage, and profiling DAX formulas, you can pinpoint areas that require optimization. Whether it involves data modeling, DAX formula simplification, or performance testing, taking these steps will ensure your reports provide a responsive and efficient user experience.

In the next section, we will delve into advanced indexing and aggregation strategies to further enhance the performance of your Power BI data models.

15.2. Indexing and Aggregation Strategies

Optimizing the performance of your Power BI data models requires careful consideration of indexing and aggregation strategies. In this section, we'll explore how these strategies can significantly enhance the responsiveness and efficiency of your reports and dashboards.

Understanding Indexing and Aggregation:

Indexing and aggregation are techniques used to streamline data retrieval and calculations in Power BI models. They help reduce the time it takes to access and process data, resulting in faster query response times.

Indexing Strategies:

1. Data Modeling Optimization:

   - Columnstore Indexes: Consider using columnstore indexes, which are highly efficient for analytical workloads. They allow for fast scanning and retrieval of data for DAX calculations.

   - Sorted Columns: Sort columns in tables, especially in large fact tables, based on commonly used filter criteria. This accelerates query performance by minimizing the number of rows to scan.

2. Aggregation Strategies:

   - Summarization: Create aggregated tables or use the SUMMARIZE function to pre-aggregate data at various granularities (e.g., daily, monthly, yearly).

   - Materialized Views: In cases of complex DAX calculations or large data models, consider using materialized views or tables that store pre-calculated values. These tables reduce the need for extensive real-time calculations.

Balancing Indexing and Aggregation:

Effective performance optimization often involves finding a balance between indexing and aggregation. Here's how you can achieve this balance:

1. Strategic Aggregation: Aggregating data at appropriate levels reduces the need for complex calculations on detailed data while speeding up queries.

2. Indexing Key Columns: Identify key columns that are frequently used in filtering and calculations and ensure they are appropriately indexed.

Example Scenario: Indexing and Aggregation

Imagine you're working on a large sales dataset, and you've noticed that sales reports are experiencing sluggish query response times. To optimize performance, you decide to create aggregated tables summarizing sales data at monthly and yearly levels. Additionally, you apply columnstore indexes to the most frequently accessed columns.

Benefits of Indexing and Aggregation:

1. Quicker Query Response: Aggregating and indexing data minimizes the time required for data retrieval and calculation, leading to faster query response times.

2. Enhanced User Experience: Users benefit from snappier and more interactive reports and dashboards.

3. Scalability: As data volumes increase, proper indexing and aggregation strategies ensure that performance remains robust.

Conclusion:

Incorporating effective indexing and aggregation strategies into your Power BI data models is a fundamental step in performance optimization. Whether it's applying columnstore indexes, creating aggregated tables, or materializing views, these techniques contribute to a more responsive and efficient reporting experience. In the next section, we will delve into query and formula optimization, which complements these strategies by fine-tuning DAX calculations for maximum efficiency.

15.3. Query and Formula Optimization

Optimizing the performance of your Power BI data models requires careful consideration of indexing and aggregation strategies. In this section, we'll explore how these strategies can significantly enhance the responsiveness and efficiency of your reports and dashboards.

Understanding Indexing and Aggregation:

Indexing and aggregation are techniques used to streamline data retrieval and calculations in Power BI models. They help reduce the time it takes to access and process data, resulting in faster query response times.

Indexing Strategies:

1. Data Modeling Optimization:

   - Columnstore Indexes: Consider using columnstore indexes, which are highly efficient for analytical workloads. They allow for fast scanning and retrieval of data for DAX calculations.

   - Sorted Columns: Sort columns in tables, especially in large fact tables, based on commonly used filter criteria. This accelerates query performance by minimizing the number of rows to scan.

2. Aggregation Strategies:

   - Summarization: Create aggregated tables or use the SUMMARIZE function to pre-aggregate data at various granularities (e.g., daily, monthly, yearly).

- Materialized Views: In cases of complex DAX calculations or large data models, consider using materialized views or tables that store pre-calculated values. These tables reduce the need for extensive real-time calculations.

Balancing Indexing and Aggregation:

Effective performance optimization often involves finding a balance between indexing and aggregation. Here's how you can achieve this balance:

1. Strategic Aggregation: Aggregating data at appropriate levels reduces the need for complex calculations on detailed data while speeding up queries.

2. Indexing Key Columns: Identify key columns that are frequently used in filtering and calculations and ensure they are appropriately indexed.

Example Scenario: Indexing and Aggregation

Imagine you're working on a large sales dataset, and you've noticed that sales reports are experiencing sluggish query response times. To optimize performance, you decide to create aggregated tables summarizing sales data at monthly and yearly levels. Additionally, you apply columnstore indexes to the most frequently accessed columns.

Benefits of Indexing and Aggregation:

1. Quicker Query Response: Aggregating and indexing data minimizes the time required for data retrieval and calculation, leading to faster query response times.

2. Enhanced User Experience: Users benefit from snappier and more interactive reports and dashboards.

3. Scalability: As data volumes increase, proper indexing and aggregation strategies ensure that performance remains robust.

Conclusion:

Incorporating effective indexing and aggregation strategies into your Power BI data models is a fundamental step in performance optimization. Whether it's applying columnstore indexes, creating aggregated tables, or materializing views, these techniques contribute to a more responsive and efficient reporting experience. In the next section, we will delve into query and formula optimization, which complements these strategies by fine-tuning DAX calculations for maximum efficiency.

Part 16. Handling Large Datasets with DAX

16.1. Data Import and Transformation for Large Data

Working with large datasets in Power BI presents unique challenges and opportunities. In this section, we'll explore strategies to efficiently import and transform large volumes of data, ensuring that your Power BI reports remain responsive and provide valuable insights.

Understanding the Challenge: Large Data Sets

Large datasets can significantly slow down report performance and limit the capabilities of your Power BI projects. These datasets often come from various sources, including databases, spreadsheets, and web services. Here's how to handle them effectively:

1. Data Source Optimization:

a. Use Query Folding: Wherever possible, leverage query folding to offload data transformation tasks to the source database. This reduces the amount of data imported into Power BI and speeds up the data retrieval process.

b. Limit Imported Columns: Import only the necessary columns from your data source. Unnecessary columns can contribute to increased data volume, affecting both performance and data model size.

2. Data Transformation Techniques:

a. Apply Filtering Early: Implement filtering operations as early as possible in your data transformation process. This ensures that irrelevant data is filtered out before it's loaded into Power BI.

b. Aggregations: Utilize aggregations to pre-calculate summary statistics for large datasets. This reduces the need for complex calculations in reports.

c. Data Sampling: When dealing with extremely large datasets, consider using data sampling techniques to work with manageable subsets. You can create meaningful reports with a smaller representative sample of data.

Memory Management Techniques:

1. Data Model Optimization: Optimize your data model by removing unused columns, minimizing calculated tables, and avoiding unnecessary relationships.

2. Compression: Power BI's VertiPaq engine provides efficient data compression. Make sure your data model benefits from this by using suitable data types and keeping data clean.

3. Distributed Data: Distribute data across multiple tables and relationships, especially for very large datasets. This can help balance the load on your data model.

Parallel Processing and Performance Scalability:

1. Partitioning: If your data source supports it, consider partitioning your data. By breaking your data into smaller, manageable partitions, you can optimize data refresh times.

2. Load Balancing: Balance the load on your Power BI service by distributing data and workloads across multiple workspaces, if available.

Example Scenario: Handling Large Sales Data

Imagine you're tasked with analyzing sales data from a retail company with millions of records. By leveraging query folding to perform data filtering at the source, aggregating key metrics in Power Query, and partitioning your data, you can significantly improve performance and maintain responsiveness in your reports.

Benefits of Data Import and Transformation for Large Data:

1. Improved Performance: By efficiently handling large datasets, your Power BI reports remain responsive, even with extensive data.

2. Scalability: The techniques mentioned allow your reports to grow with your data without compromising performance.

3. Resource Efficiency: By importing and transforming only necessary data, you save resources and ensure a smoother reporting experience.

Conclusion:

Handling large datasets in Power BI is a crucial skill for advanced data modeling. By optimizing data sources, applying efficient transformation techniques, and managing memory wisely, you can create robust and high-performing reports that provide valuable insights from vast amounts of data. In this part of the book, you've learned how to handle large datasets and lay the foundation for mastering DAX in Power BI.

16.2. Memory Management Techniques

Efficient memory management is essential when dealing with large datasets in Power BI. In this section, we'll explore various techniques to optimize memory usage, ensuring your Power BI reports run smoothly and provide a responsive user experience.

Understanding the Importance of Memory Management:

When working with large datasets, Power BI's memory utilization becomes critical. Inadequate memory management can lead to sluggish report performance and limit the scalability of your projects. Here's how to effectively manage memory:

1. Data Model Optimization:

   a. Column Pruning: One of the key techniques in memory management is to prune unnecessary columns. In your data model, you should only include the columns that are essential for your analysis. Exclude any extraneous or duplicate columns to reduce memory usage.

   b. Data Type Optimization: Utilize appropriate data types for your columns. For example, use integer data types instead of floating-point numbers if the precision isn't required. This optimization minimizes the memory footprint of your data model.

2. Aggregations:

a. Pre-Aggregated Tables: Implement pre-aggregated tables in your data model. These tables store summary statistics and calculations, reducing the need for complex aggregations at query time. They are particularly useful for large datasets with frequent aggregation requirements.

b. Summarization within DAX: Take advantage of DAX functions like SUMMARIZE, SUMMARIZECOLUMNS, and ADDCOLUMNS to create summarized tables in DAX. These tables can simplify your measures and reduce memory consumption.

3. Memory Usage Monitoring:

a. Performance Analyzer: Utilize the Performance Analyzer tool in Power BI to monitor memory usage. It helps identify which visuals and DAX calculations consume the most memory, allowing you to optimize specific areas of your report.

b. Resource Monitor: Keep an eye on the Power BI Service's resource monitor to check your report's memory footprint in the cloud environment.

4. Limiting Visuals and Rows:

a. Data Slicers: Use data slicers or filters to limit the data displayed in visuals. Only loading the necessary data can significantly reduce memory usage.

b. Top N Filtering: Implement Top N filtering in visuals to display a limited number of items, which is especially helpful in reports with vast datasets.

5. Managing Data Refresh:

a. Incremental Refresh: Implement incremental data refresh strategies to load only the most recent data into your data model. This is crucial for reports that connect to large and frequently updated datasets.

Example Scenario: Optimizing a Large Inventory Dataset

Imagine you're working with a massive inventory dataset for a retail company. By meticulously pruning unnecessary columns, optimizing data types, and creating pre-aggregated tables for common metrics like total sales, you can ensure that your report remains responsive even with millions of inventory records.

Benefits of Memory Management Techniques:

1. Improved Performance: Efficient memory management ensures that your Power BI reports load quickly and provide a responsive user experience, even with extensive datasets.

2. Scalability: These techniques allow your reports to scale with your data without compromising performance.

3. Resource Efficiency: By optimizing memory usage, you conserve resources, which is especially crucial for the Power BI Service.

Conclusion:

Memory management is a fundamental aspect of optimizing large datasets in Power BI. By implementing the memory management techniques discussed in this section, you can create high-performance reports that deliver valuable insights from substantial datasets while maintaining a responsive user experience. This knowledge is essential for mastering DAX in Power BI and achieving excellence in data modeling.

16.3. Parallel Processing and Performance Scalability

When handling large datasets in Power BI, achieving optimal performance can be a challenge. Parallel processing and scalability are crucial strategies to ensure that your reports remain responsive and efficient as your data grows. In this section, we'll explore how to implement parallel processing and improve the scalability of your Power BI solutions.

Understanding Parallel Processing:

Parallel processing is a technique where multiple tasks are executed simultaneously rather than sequentially. In Power BI, this means distributing data processing tasks across available resources to reduce overall execution time. It's especially valuable for large datasets where traditional sequential processing can be time-consuming.

Key Concepts for Parallel Processing:

1. Multi-Core Processors: Utilize multi-core processors effectively. Power BI can take advantage of multiple CPU cores for parallel data processing.

2. Distributed Data: Distribute your data across multiple tables or partitions. Each table or partition can be processed in parallel, significantly improving performance.

3. Data Splitting: Divide data into smaller, manageable chunks. For example, if you have a large fact table, consider partitioning it into smaller time-based or category-based partitions.

Improving Scalability:

Scalability is the ability to handle an increasing amount of data while maintaining performance. Achieving scalability in Power BI involves a combination of strategies, including data modeling, indexing, and data partitioning.

Partitioning Data: Partitioning your data involves splitting it into smaller, more manageable pieces, typically based on a particular attribute or timeframe. For example, if you have several years of sales data, partition it into individual yearly or quarterly tables. This approach allows Power BI to read and refresh only the necessary partitions, reducing data load times and improving report performance.

Parallel Data Processing: When your dataset is partitioned, Power BI can leverage parallel processing. Each partition is processed separately, utilizing available CPU cores. This can dramatically reduce data refresh times, making your reports more responsive.

Scalable Data Modeling: Design your data model with scalability in mind. Use efficient relationships, aggregated tables, and partitioning to ensure your reports can handle larger datasets without performance degradation.

Example Scenario: Improving Scalability with Parallel Processing

Consider a retail company with a growing volume of sales data. By partitioning their fact table into smaller, monthly tables, they can improve data refresh times. Additionally, the utilization of parallel processing ensures that data from each monthly table is processed simultaneously, resulting in faster report performance.

Benefits of Parallel Processing and Scalability:

1. Faster Data Refresh: Parallel processing reduces the time it takes to refresh your data, ensuring that your reports are up to date more quickly.

2. Responsive Reports: Scalability and parallel processing lead to more responsive reports, even as your datasets expand.

3. Improved User Experience: Users can interact with your reports without encountering performance issues, enhancing their experience.

4. Efficient Resource Usage: These techniques allow you to make efficient use of available system resources, including CPU cores and memory.

Conclusion:

Parallel processing and scalability are essential for handling large datasets in Power BI. By leveraging these techniques and best practices, you can ensure that your reports remain efficient, responsive, and capable of accommodating growing volumes of data. These concepts are fundamental to mastering DAX and achieving advanced data modeling in Power BI.

CHAPTER VII
Advanced Case Studies

Part 17. Advanced Case Study 1: E-commerce Analytics

17.1. Sales and Inventory Analysis

In this case study, we delve into the world of e-commerce analytics, focusing on sales and inventory analysis using Power BI and advanced DAX techniques. We'll explore how to gain insights into your e-commerce business, optimize inventory management, and make data-driven decisions to improve sales performance.

Understanding the Challenge:

E-commerce businesses face the continuous challenge of optimizing inventory to meet customer demand, minimizing overstock and understock situations, and enhancing sales performance. Traditional data analysis approaches can fall short in providing real-time insights and making dynamic decisions. This is where Power BI and DAX come into play.

Key Objectives:

1. Sales Performance Analysis: Understand your sales trends, identify top-performing products, and explore sales patterns over time.

2. Inventory Optimization: Ensure that inventory levels are aligned with customer demand while minimizing carrying costs.

3. Real-time Insights: Leverage the power of Power BI to access real-time data and insights for proactive decision-making.

Data Modeling and Preparation:

To perform effective sales and inventory analysis, you need a well-structured data model. Here are some key considerations:

- Data Integration: Combine your sales data with inventory data to get a comprehensive view of your e-commerce operations.

- Time Intelligence: Implement time intelligence functions in DAX to enable comparisons over different time periods, such as year-over-year sales comparisons.

- Calculations: Develop custom DAX calculations for key performance indicators (KPIs) like sell-through rate, inventory turnover, and gross margin.

Sales Analysis:

- Sales Trends: Use line charts and time-based DAX functions to visualize sales trends. Identify peak selling seasons, understand monthly or weekly sales patterns, and plan your inventory accordingly.

- Top-Performing Products: Utilize DAX measures to identify best-selling products, top revenue generators, and products that contribute most to profit margins.

- Customer Segmentation: Segment your customer base using DAX functions. Understand the preferences and behaviors of different customer groups.

Inventory Analysis:

- Inventory Turnover: Calculate inventory turnover rates to understand how quickly products are sold. High turnover indicates efficient inventory management.

- Safety Stock: Implement safety stock calculations to maintain a buffer of inventory for unexpected demand spikes.

- Overstock/Understock Alerts: Use DAX to set up alerts for overstock and understock situations, enabling proactive action.

Real-time Reporting:

Power BI's real-time capabilities enable you to monitor sales and inventory data as it happens. Implement real-time dashboards and reports that provide immediate insights into sales trends, inventory status, and customer behavior.

Example Scenario: Sales and Inventory Analysis

Consider an e-commerce business that sells electronic gadgets. By implementing Power BI and advanced DAX measures, the company can identify its best-selling products, track inventory turnover rates, and optimize stocking levels for each product category. Real-time alerts for low inventory levels help them proactively restock popular items, ensuring customer satisfaction and increased sales.

Conclusion:

Sales and inventory analysis in e-commerce is vital for maintaining a competitive edge. Power BI and advanced DAX techniques empower businesses to make data-driven decisions, optimize inventory management, and boost sales performance. By mastering these techniques, you can elevate your e-commerce analytics to a new level of effectiveness and efficiency.

17.2. Customer Behavior and Recommendations

In this case study, we'll explore the fascinating world of customer behavior analysis and recommendations within the context of e-commerce analytics. By harnessing the power of Power BI and advanced DAX techniques, you can gain a deeper understanding of your customers and provide personalized product recommendations to enhance their shopping experience.

Understanding the Challenge:

Understanding customer behavior and providing tailored product recommendations is essential for e-commerce success. In a highly competitive online marketplace, businesses must go beyond traditional sales strategies and provide a personalized shopping experience. This is where Power BI and advanced DAX calculations play a pivotal role.

Key Objectives:

1. Customer Segmentation: Use DAX functions to segment your customer base. Identify different customer groups based on purchase history, demographics, and browsing behavior.

2. Behavior Analysis: Dive deep into customer behavior by analyzing factors like frequency of purchases, average order value, and browsing patterns.

3. Personalized Recommendations: Leverage DAX measures and algorithms to offer customers personalized product recommendations, increasing cross-selling and upselling opportunities.

Data Modeling and Preparation:

To unlock the power of customer behavior analysis and recommendations, your data model should be well-structured:

- Customer Data Integration: Integrate customer data with transactional data to create a comprehensive dataset.

- Customer Segmentation: Develop DAX calculations that assign customers to segments based on their behavior and attributes.

- Recommendation Engine: Implement DAX functions for building a recommendation engine. Collaborative filtering and item-based filtering techniques can be particularly useful.

Customer Behavior Analysis:

- Customer Segmentation: Create dynamic customer segments using DAX functions. For example, segment customers into new, returning, and high-value customer groups.

- Behavior Metrics: Utilize DAX to calculate various behavior metrics, including purchase frequency, recency, and average purchase value. Visualize these metrics with Power BI visuals.

- Churn Prediction: Use DAX to create a churn prediction model. Identify customers at risk of churning and take proactive measures to retain them.

Personalized Recommendations:

- Collaborative Filtering: Implement collaborative filtering algorithms in DAX to provide personalized product recommendations based on user behavior and preferences.

- Item-Based Filtering: Develop item-based filtering in DAX to recommend products similar to those a customer has previously purchased or shown interest in.

Real-world Example: Customer Behavior and Recommendations

Consider an online fashion retailer. By implementing Power BI and advanced DAX measures, the retailer can segment customers into various groups, such as occasional shoppers, frequent buyers, and fashion enthusiasts. They can then provide personalized clothing recommendations based on the customer's shopping history and preferences. These recommendations increase customer engagement and boost sales.

Conclusion:

Understanding customer behavior and providing personalized recommendations is crucial in today's e-commerce landscape. By mastering the use of Power BI and advanced DAX techniques, you can delve into customer behavior, offer tailored recommendations, and elevate your e-commerce analytics to new heights. This not only enhances the customer experience but also leads to increased sales and customer loyalty.

17.3. Fraud Detection and Prevention

In this advanced case study, we will delve into the critical realm of fraud detection and prevention using Power BI and advanced DAX modeling techniques. As online transactions and e-commerce continue to grow, the need to safeguard against fraudulent activities becomes paramount. Power BI, combined with DAX calculations, provides a robust solution for detecting and preventing fraud in real-time.

Understanding the Challenge:

Fraud detection is a complex task, especially in e-commerce. Fraudsters continually adapt their methods, making it crucial for businesses to stay one step ahead. The challenge lies in identifying fraudulent patterns within vast datasets, requiring not only advanced algorithms but also real-time monitoring.

Key Objectives:

1. Real-time Monitoring: Utilize DAX calculations to enable real-time monitoring of transactions, identifying anomalies and patterns associated with fraudulent activities.

2. Fraud Risk Assessment: Develop DAX models to assess the risk associated with each transaction and customer, flagging those with a higher likelihood of being fraudulent.

3. Visualization and Alerts: Implement Power BI dashboards to visualize and track fraud indicators. Set up automated alerts for immediate action.

Data Modeling and Preparation:

To effectively detect and prevent fraud, a well-structured data model is vital:

- Transaction Data: Integrate transaction data and customer information. Ensure data integrity and consistency.

- Feature Engineering: Create DAX calculations to engineer features that highlight potentially fraudulent activities, such as unusual purchase locations, transaction frequencies, and order sizes.

- Machine Learning Integration: Combine DAX with machine learning models to improve fraud prediction accuracy.

Real-time Fraud Detection:

- Advanced DAX Calculations: Employ DAX to calculate risk scores and fraud indicators based on historical and real-time data.

- Behavior Pattern Recognition: Utilize DAX measures to recognize patterns in customer behavior and transaction history that could indicate fraud.

- Automated Alerts: Set up DAX-driven automated alerts for potential fraudulent activities. For example, if a transaction exceeds a defined risk threshold, an alert is generated.

Example: Real-time Fraud Detection

Consider an e-commerce platform that leverages Power BI and advanced DAX calculations. Using real-time data, the system assesses each transaction's risk based on factors like location, purchase history, and the customer's behavior. If a transaction is flagged as high-risk due to suspicious patterns, an automated alert is sent to the security team for immediate review. This proactive approach helps prevent fraudulent activities before they impact the business.

Conclusion:

Fraud detection and prevention are paramount for e-commerce businesses. Power BI, in conjunction with advanced DAX modeling techniques, offers a robust solution. By creating real-time monitoring, risk assessment, and automated alerting systems, you can stay ahead of fraudsters and protect your business and customers. This case study highlights the application of DAX for enhancing fraud detection and prevention in the e-commerce sector.

Part 18. Advanced Case Study 2: Supply Chain Optimization

18.1. Inventory and Demand Forecasting

In this advanced case study, we will explore the application of Power BI and advanced DAX modeling techniques in the domain of supply chain optimization. Specifically, we will focus on the critical aspects of inventory management and demand forecasting. These are essential components of a well-functioning supply chain, as they enable businesses to optimize inventory levels, reduce carrying costs, and ensure that products are available to meet customer demand.

The Significance of Inventory and Demand Forecasting:

Inventory management and demand forecasting are pivotal for businesses across various industries, such as retail, manufacturing, and distribution. The key objectives are to:

1. Minimize Costs: Keep inventory carrying costs low by optimizing stock levels to meet anticipated demand without overstocking.

2. Improve Customer Satisfaction: Ensure products are available when customers need them, leading to increased customer satisfaction and sales.

3. Predictive Analytics: Leverage advanced DAX modeling to analyze historical data and develop predictive models that anticipate future demand accurately.

Data Preparation and Integration:

Effective inventory and demand forecasting begins with robust data preparation and integration:

- Historical Sales Data: Collect and integrate historical sales data, including details like product types, quantities sold, and timeframes.

- External Factors: Consider external factors that influence demand, such as seasonality, promotions, or economic conditions.

- Data Cleaning: Clean and preprocess data to remove outliers and ensure consistency.

Advanced DAX Techniques:

The power of DAX comes into play in developing accurate demand forecasting models:

- Time Intelligence Functions: Utilize DAX's time intelligence functions to analyze trends over time, identify seasonality, and apply rolling averages.

- Predictive Models: Implement predictive models in Power BI using DAX functions to forecast future demand. Techniques like Exponential Smoothing, ARIMA, or machine learning can be integrated.

- Visualization: Create interactive visualizations in Power BI to display historical sales data, forecasts, and relevant KPIs.

Example: Demand Forecasting Model

Imagine a manufacturing company that uses Power BI and advanced DAX modeling techniques for demand forecasting. By analyzing historical sales data, implementing predictive models, and visualizing the results in Power BI dashboards, the company achieves more accurate demand forecasts. As a result, they can adjust production schedules, inventory levels, and supplier orders in real-time, ensuring products are readily available to meet customer demand without overstocking.

Conclusion:

Inventory and demand forecasting are indispensable for optimizing the supply chain and enhancing overall business performance. This case study illustrates the application of advanced DAX modeling techniques in Power BI to improve inventory management and demand forecasting accuracy. By leveraging historical data and advanced analytics, businesses can make informed decisions and keep inventory costs in check while satisfying customer demand.

18.2. Supplier Performance Metrics

In this advanced case study, we delve into the realm of supply chain optimization and explore the critical aspect of evaluating and enhancing supplier performance. Supplier performance metrics are instrumental in ensuring that your supply chain operates efficiently and cost-effectively by maintaining strong relationships with your suppliers.

The Importance of Supplier Performance Metrics:

The performance of your suppliers has a direct impact on your organization's ability to meet customer demand and manage costs. Effective supplier performance metrics help businesses:

1. Quality Assurance: Ensure that the materials or products supplied by vendors meet the required quality standards.

2. On-time Delivery: Monitor and improve delivery schedules to prevent production delays or stockouts.

3. Cost Efficiency: Negotiate favorable terms and pricing with suppliers, reducing operational costs.

Key Supplier Performance Metrics:

Effective supplier performance metrics encompass a range of key indicators that provide insights into supplier performance. Some of these metrics include:

- On-time Delivery Performance: Evaluate the percentage of orders delivered on time against the total number of orders.

- Quality Metrics: Assess product quality through criteria such as defect rates, rejection rates, or customer returns.

- Cost Metrics: Analyze cost-related metrics, including price variance, cost of goods sold (COGS), and cost-saving initiatives.

Data Integration and Analysis:

To implement supplier performance metrics in Power BI, you need to:

- Data Integration: Integrate data sources related to supplier performance, including purchase orders, delivery records, quality assurance reports, and financial data.

- Data Cleaning: Cleanse and preprocess the data to ensure accuracy and consistency.

- Advanced DAX Calculations: Utilize DAX functions to calculate supplier performance metrics. For instance, calculate the on-time delivery rate, defect rates, and cost variances.

- Data Visualization: Create intuitive dashboards and reports in Power BI to visualize the supplier performance metrics. Use visuals like scorecards, KPI indicators, and drill-through reports.

Example: On-time Delivery Performance Metrics

Suppose a manufacturing company relies on multiple suppliers for raw materials. By implementing supplier performance metrics in Power BI, the company can track the on-time delivery performance of each supplier over time. The Power BI dashboard displays each supplier's on-time delivery rate, highlighting areas for improvement. This enables the company to make data-driven decisions on supplier selection, negotiations, and risk mitigation.

Conclusion:

Supplier performance metrics are essential in optimizing the supply chain by ensuring that suppliers meet quality, delivery, and cost efficiency requirements. This case study demonstrates how to implement supplier performance metrics in Power BI using advanced DAX modeling techniques. By tracking key metrics and visualizing supplier performance, businesses can foster strong supplier relationships and improve overall supply chain efficiency.

18.3. Logistics and Distribution Analytics

In this advanced case study on supply chain optimization, we explore the vital area of logistics and distribution analytics. Efficient logistics and distribution processes are fundamental to ensuring that products and materials move seamlessly through the supply chain, ultimately reaching customers in a timely and cost-effective manner.

The Significance of Logistics and Distribution Analytics:

Logistics and distribution analytics play a pivotal role in supply chain management by providing insights and optimizing the flow of goods. These analytics offer several benefits, including:

1. Cost Reduction: Identify areas for cost savings by optimizing transportation, warehousing, and inventory management.

2. Service Improvement: Enhance customer satisfaction by ensuring timely deliveries and accurate order fulfillment.

3. Risk Mitigation: Identify potential disruptions and implement contingency plans to minimize supply chain risks.

Key Logistics and Distribution Analytics:

Effective logistics and distribution analytics encompass a range of key performance indicators and metrics, such as:

- Route Optimization: Analyze the most efficient routes for transportation to reduce fuel costs and delivery times.

- Inventory Turnover: Measure how quickly inventory is sold or used, optimizing the balance between stock availability and carrying costs.

- Warehouse Efficiency: Assess the efficiency of warehousing operations, including storage utilization, picking accuracy, and labor productivity.

Data Integration and Analysis:

To implement logistics and distribution analytics in Power BI, you need to:

- Data Integration: Integrate various data sources, such as transportation data, order records, inventory data, and customer feedback.

- Data Cleansing: Cleanse and preprocess data to ensure data quality and consistency.

- Advanced DAX Calculations: Utilize DAX functions to create calculations like route optimization, inventory turnover rates, and warehouse efficiency metrics.

- Data Visualization: Develop Power BI dashboards that provide clear insights into logistics and distribution. Utilize visuals such as maps, Gantt charts, and bar charts to present the analytics effectively.

Example: Route Optimization

Suppose a distribution company manages a fleet of vehicles for delivering products to customers. By implementing logistics and distribution analytics in Power BI, the company can optimize routes based on factors like distance, traffic conditions, and delivery time windows. The Power BI dashboard provides route recommendations and monitors vehicle performance. This results in reduced fuel costs, faster deliveries, and increased customer satisfaction.

Conclusion:

Logistics and distribution analytics are indispensable for enhancing the efficiency of supply chain operations. In this case study, we demonstrate how to leverage Power BI and DAX modeling to implement logistics and distribution analytics effectively. By analyzing key performance indicators and visualizing the data, businesses can make informed decisions, reduce costs, and improve the overall logistics and distribution processes.

Part 19. Advanced Case Study 3: Healthcare Analytics

19.1. Patient Outcomes Analysis

In our advanced case study on healthcare analytics, we delve into the crucial domain of patient outcomes analysis. This application of Power BI and DAX modeling is instrumental in the healthcare industry, as it empowers healthcare providers and organizations to evaluate and enhance the quality of care they deliver to patients. Patient outcomes analysis focuses on assessing the impact of treatments, procedures, and healthcare interventions on patients' health and well-being.

Importance of Patient Outcomes Analysis:

Patient outcomes analysis holds immense significance in the healthcare field for several reasons:

1. Quality Improvement: By analyzing patient outcomes, healthcare providers can identify areas for improvement in clinical practices, which can lead to enhanced patient care.

2. Cost Reduction: Understanding which treatments yield the best outcomes allows for more cost-effective allocation of resources and the avoidance of unnecessary expenses.

3. Evidence-Based Decision-Making: It enables healthcare organizations to make decisions based on empirical data and patient feedback rather than relying solely on intuition.

Key Aspects of Patient Outcomes Analysis:

Patient outcomes analysis involves a range of key metrics and elements, including:

- Mortality Rates: Examining the rates at which patients pass away during treatment or after specific medical procedures.

- Rehospitalization Rates: Assessing how often patients need to be readmitted for the same or related conditions after an initial treatment.

- Patient Satisfaction Scores: Gauging patient satisfaction with their overall healthcare experience.

Data Integration and Analysis:

Implementing patient outcomes analysis in Power BI necessitates the following steps:

- Data Integration: Incorporate data from various sources, including electronic health records (EHRs), patient surveys, clinical databases, and more.

- Data Preparation: Cleanse, transform, and prepare the data for analysis. This includes handling missing data, normalizing data, and ensuring data accuracy.

- Advanced DAX Modeling: Employ DAX functions to create calculations for patient outcomes metrics. For example, calculating mortality rates, rehospitalization rates, and satisfaction scores.

- Data Visualization: Develop comprehensive Power BI dashboards with visuals such as line charts, bar charts, and heatmaps to effectively present patient outcomes data.

Example: Mortality Rates Analysis

Consider a hospital aiming to analyze the mortality rates associated with a specific medical procedure. By using Power BI and DAX modeling, the hospital can import data on patient outcomes, calculate mortality rates, and visualize trends over time. This analysis allows the hospital to identify areas where mortality rates are higher and make informed decisions to enhance patient care and reduce risks.

Conclusion:

Patient outcomes analysis is a pivotal aspect of healthcare analytics, guiding healthcare providers in optimizing their services and treatment methods. In this case study, we've demonstrated how to apply Power BI and DAX modeling to assess and improve patient outcomes. The use of empirical data and the visualization of key metrics empower healthcare organizations to make data-driven decisions, leading to enhanced patient care and cost-effective practices.

19.2. Medical Costs and Billing Analytics

In this advanced case study on healthcare analytics, we explore the critical domain of medical costs and billing analytics using Power BI and DAX modeling. Understanding and managing medical costs, as well as optimizing billing processes, are pivotal aspects of healthcare administration. Healthcare organizations and providers can leverage data-driven insights to control expenses, improve billing accuracy, and ensure financial sustainability.

Importance of Medical Costs and Billing Analytics:

Medical costs and billing analytics play a crucial role in healthcare for various reasons:

1. Cost Control: Healthcare organizations need to manage and control expenses to provide high-quality care while remaining financially sustainable.

2. Billing Accuracy: Accurate and efficient billing processes are essential for revenue generation and maintaining financial health.

3. Regulatory Compliance: Compliance with healthcare regulations and insurance requirements is vital to avoid legal issues and fines.

Key Aspects of Medical Costs and Billing Analytics:

Medical costs and billing analytics involve several key components:

- Cost Analysis: Evaluating the costs associated with various medical procedures, treatments, and services.

- Revenue Analysis: Understanding the sources of revenue, such as insurance reimbursements and patient payments.

- Billing Efficiency: Assessing the efficiency of billing processes, including claims processing and coding accuracy.

- Compliance Monitoring: Ensuring that billing practices adhere to healthcare regulations and insurance guidelines.

Data Integration and Analysis:

To implement medical costs and billing analytics in Power BI, follow these steps:

- Data Aggregation: Collect and aggregate data from multiple sources, including billing systems, electronic health records (EHRs), and insurance claims.

- Data Transformation: Cleanse, normalize, and prepare the data for analysis to ensure accuracy and consistency.

- DAX Modeling: Utilize DAX functions to create calculations for cost analysis, revenue tracking, and billing efficiency.

- Data Visualization: Develop interactive Power BI dashboards with visuals like pie charts, bar graphs, and tables to present financial and billing data effectively.

Example: Cost Analysis for a Medical Procedure

Imagine a healthcare organization wanting to analyze the cost of performing a specific medical procedure. By using Power BI and DAX modeling, they can integrate data related to personnel, equipment, supplies, and overhead costs. They can then use DAX functions to calculate the total cost per procedure and create visualizations that help identify opportunities to reduce costs or improve efficiency.

Conclusion:

Medical costs and billing analytics are essential for maintaining the financial health of healthcare organizations. In this case study, we have demonstrated how Power BI and DAX modeling can be applied to analyze and optimize medical costs and billing processes. By gaining insights into expenses, revenues, and billing efficiency, healthcare providers can make informed decisions to enhance financial sustainability and compliance.

19.3. Clinical Trials and Drug Development

In this advanced case study on healthcare analytics, we delve into the vital domain of clinical trials and drug development, demonstrating how Power BI and DAX modeling can offer valuable insights and optimization capabilities. Clinical trials are an integral part of the pharmaceutical and healthcare industries, aimed at evaluating the safety and effectiveness of new drugs and treatments. Effective data analysis plays a critical role in streamlining the drug development process.

Importance of Clinical Trials and Drug Development Analytics:

Clinical trials and drug development analytics are of paramount importance for the following reasons:

1. Safety and Efficacy Assessment: Clinical trials assess the safety and efficacy of new drugs or treatments before they are approved for widespread use.

2. Regulatory Compliance: Adherence to regulatory requirements is crucial to ensure the validity of clinical trial results and compliance with industry standards.

3. Cost Efficiency: Efficient data analysis and modeling can reduce the cost and duration of clinical trials, which are often resource-intensive.

Key Aspects of Clinical Trials and Drug Development Analytics:

Effective analysis in this domain includes various aspects:

- Patient Recruitment: Identifying and recruiting suitable candidates for clinical trials.

- Clinical Trial Design: Designing trials with appropriate endpoints, sample sizes, and protocols.

- Data Collection: Gathering and recording data on patient outcomes, side effects, and treatment effectiveness.

- Regulatory Reporting: Compiling and submitting data to regulatory authorities for approval.

Data Integration and Analysis:

To implement clinical trials and drug development analytics in Power BI, follow these steps:

- Data Integration: Collect and integrate data from various sources, including clinical records, patient data, and regulatory databases.

- Data Transformation: Clean and prepare the data for analysis, ensuring data consistency and accuracy.

- DAX Modeling: Utilize DAX functions to create calculations for patient recruitment, trial design, and regulatory reporting.

- Data Visualization: Develop informative Power BI dashboards with visuals such as line charts, scatter plots, and tables to present trial data effectively.

Example: Patient Recruitment Optimization

Imagine a pharmaceutical company aiming to optimize patient recruitment for a clinical trial. By using Power BI and DAX modeling, they can integrate data on patient profiles, medical history, and trial eligibility criteria. DAX calculations can help identify target patient populations and optimize recruitment strategies. Visualizations in Power BI can provide insights into the recruitment process, highlighting areas for improvement and efficiency gains.

Conclusion:

Clinical trials and drug development analytics are pivotal in the pharmaceutical and healthcare sectors. In this case study, we have demonstrated how Power BI and DAX modeling can be applied to streamline the clinical trial process. By optimizing patient recruitment, trial design, and regulatory compliance, healthcare and pharmaceutical professionals can expedite drug development while ensuring patient safety and adherence to regulatory standards.

CHAPTER VIII
Future Trends and Beyond

Part 20. Emerging Trends in DAX and Power BI

20.1. Artificial Intelligence and Machine Learning Integration

In the rapidly evolving landscape of data analytics, the integration of Artificial Intelligence (AI) and Machine Learning (ML) with Power BI and DAX modeling is a profound development. This chapter explores how these technologies are transforming the way organizations harness data and insights, enhancing the capabilities of Power BI.

The Intersection of Power BI, DAX, AI, and ML:

The integration of AI and ML into Power BI extends its capabilities, enabling organizations to unlock deeper insights and predictions from their data. By harnessing the synergy of Power BI's data modeling capabilities and AI/ML algorithms, a myriad of applications are made possible.

Applications and Use Cases:

1. Data Predictions: AI and ML models can be used to predict future data trends, helping organizations make informed decisions. For example, a retail company can use ML algorithms to forecast sales figures based on historical data, seasonality, and external factors.

2. Anomaly Detection: AI-driven anomaly detection can automatically identify unusual data patterns or outliers, aiding in fraud detection, network security, or quality control.

3. Natural Language Processing (NLP): Integration with NLP allows users to perform text analysis and sentiment analysis within Power BI. This is particularly valuable for extracting insights from customer feedback, reviews, or social media data.

4. Recommendation Systems: ML algorithms can power recommendation engines that provide personalized product recommendations to e-commerce customers or suggest content for media platforms.

Data Preparation and Modeling:

To effectively integrate AI and ML with Power BI, several steps are involved:

- Data Preparation: Data must be cleansed, transformed, and structured properly. DAX modeling techniques are still pivotal for preparing the data for AI/ML.

- Model Building: AI/ML models must be constructed or trained based on the nature of the problem. Common tools like Python or R can be used in conjunction with Power BI to build models.

- Integration: The AI/ML models are integrated into Power BI, allowing for real-time or batch predictions and analysis.

Example: Customer Churn Prediction

Imagine a telecommunications company seeking to reduce customer churn. They can use Power BI to create a comprehensive customer dataset that includes demographic information, usage patterns, and customer service interactions. With the integration of AI and ML, they develop a churn prediction model that identifies customers at risk of leaving. Power BI dashboards can then display these insights, enabling the company to take proactive retention measures.

The Future of AI and ML Integration:

As AI and ML continue to advance, their integration with Power BI will only become more sophisticated. Organizations will benefit from more automated insights, real-time predictions, and enhanced natural language understanding, driving data-driven decision-making to new heights.

20.2. Real-Time Data Analysis

In the ever-evolving landscape of data analysis and visualization, real-time data analysis stands as one of the most pivotal and transformative trends. This chapter delves into how Power BI, with its robust DAX modeling capabilities, is adapting to cater to the increasing demand for real-time insights.

The Essence of Real-Time Data Analysis:

Real-time data analysis, often referred to as streaming analytics, is the process of continuously processing and analyzing data as it's generated, allowing organizations to make decisions, respond to events, and identify trends immediately. This is particularly crucial in industries where timely insights can be a game-changer.

Applications and Use Cases:

1. Financial Services: In stock trading, real-time data analysis allows traders to make split-second decisions based on market fluctuations and relevant news.

2. IoT and Manufacturing: In manufacturing, IoT sensors continuously transmit data on machine performance, helping to predict maintenance needs and optimize production.

3. E-commerce: E-commerce platforms use real-time analysis to track website traffic, user behavior, and adjust product recommendations in real-time.

4. Social Media: Social media platforms employ real-time analysis to monitor trends, user interactions, and respond to viral content or potential issues promptly.

Real-Time Data in Power BI:

Power BI is adapting to the real-time trend with the introduction of real-time data streaming and continuous refresh capabilities. Data connectors, such as those for Azure Stream Analytics, allow users to connect to real-time data sources.

Example: Stock Market Analysis

Let's consider an example of real-time data analysis in Power BI. An investment firm leverages Power BI's real-time capabilities to monitor stock market data. They create a dashboard that displays real-time stock prices, price fluctuations, and the latest financial news. This enables their financial analysts to react swiftly to market changes and make informed investment decisions.

The Future of Real-Time Data Analysis:

Real-time data analysis will continue to evolve, offering even more complex and interactive capabilities. Power BI is expected to further enhance its real-time data analysis features, providing more sophisticated data connectors, improved performance, and advanced visualizations. The ability to harness real-time insights will become a standard requirement for data analysts in various industries.

20.3. Mobile and Cloud Solutions

Mobile and cloud solutions have revolutionized the way data is accessed, shared, and analyzed. Power BI is at the forefront of adapting to these trends, making it easier than ever for users to access their data anytime, anywhere.

The Mobility Revolution:

The proliferation of smartphones and tablets has transformed how we interact with data. Mobile devices are no longer just for communication; they are powerful tools for data consumption and decision-making. As such, Power BI has adapted to this shift by optimizing its platform for mobile use.

Mobile Features in Power BI:

Power BI offers a range of features that cater to mobile users, ensuring they can access and interact with data efficiently:

1. Responsive Design: Reports and dashboards created in Power BI are designed to be responsive, automatically adjusting to different screen sizes and orientations.

2. Mobile Apps: Power BI provides mobile apps for iOS and Android, allowing users to access their reports and dashboards on the go.

3. Offline Access: Mobile users can download reports for offline access, ensuring they have critical data available even when not connected to the internet.

4. Touch-Optimized Interactivity: Reports are designed with touch screen devices in mind, allowing users to interact with visualizations using touch gestures.

Example: Sales Dashboard for Field Representatives

Imagine a sales organization where field representatives are continually on the move, meeting clients and prospects. To support their activities, the company uses Power BI's mobile features to provide a sales dashboard accessible via the mobile app. This dashboard displays real-time sales data, client information, and inventory levels. Representatives can access this information even when they're out of the office, enabling them to provide better-informed recommendations and close deals more effectively.

The Power of the Cloud:

Cloud solutions have redefined data storage, analysis, and collaboration. Power BI leverages the cloud in several ways to provide flexibility and scalability.

Cloud Features in Power BI:

1. Power BI Service: The cloud-based Power BI service allows users to publish and share reports and dashboards with colleagues, clients, or the public securely.

2. Data Storage: Power BI can connect to various cloud-based data sources, including Azure, OneDrive, and SharePoint, making it convenient to work with data stored in the cloud.

3. Collaboration: Power BI provides collaboration features such as real-time sharing, comments, and annotations, allowing teams to collaborate effectively.

Example: Collaborative Budgeting

A financial services firm uses Power BI's cloud features to streamline its budgeting process. Multiple teams across various locations collaborate on budget proposals in real-time using Power BI Service. They can access, edit, and comment on budget reports simultaneously, ensuring a transparent and efficient budgeting process.

The Future of Mobile and Cloud Solutions in Power BI:

Mobile and cloud solutions are poised to play an increasingly significant role in the Power BI ecosystem. As mobile devices become more powerful and cloud technologies advance, Power BI will likely introduce more innovative features and integrations, making it an indispensable tool for organizations looking to harness data insights anytime and anywhere.

Part 21. Preparing for the Future of Data Modeling

21.1. Data Governance and Compliance

In an era where data is the lifeblood of organizations, ensuring proper data governance and compliance is imperative. Data governance encompasses the framework, processes, and policies for managing data quality, security, privacy, and compliance with regulations. With Power BI's extensive capabilities, you can uphold robust data governance practices within your organization.

The Significance of Data Governance:

Data governance is critical for maintaining data quality, consistency, and trustworthiness. It ensures that data is accurate, secure, and complies with relevant regulations, such as GDPR, HIPAA, or industry-specific requirements. Proper data governance safeguards your organization against data breaches, legal issues, and reputational damage.

Key Aspects of Data Governance in Power BI:

Power BI offers tools and features to facilitate data governance and compliance, making it a trustworthy platform for organizations dealing with sensitive and regulated data.

1. Data Classification and Sensitivity Labels: Power BI allows you to classify data and apply sensitivity labels to identify data that requires specific protection. This helps in ensuring that sensitive data is handled appropriately.

2. Data Lineage: Understanding data lineage is vital for tracing the origin of data and its transformation journey within Power BI. This feature aids in auditing and compliance reporting.

3. Data Refresh Schedules: Power BI enables organizations to control the frequency and timing of data refreshes, which can be crucial for compliance with regulations that require specific data retention periods.

4. Data Security: Power BI offers role-level security to restrict access to data based on users' roles and permissions. This ensures that only authorized personnel can view sensitive information.

5. Audit Logs: Power BI keeps comprehensive audit logs to track user activity, providing insights into who accessed what data, and when. These logs are invaluable for compliance audits.

Example: GDPR Compliance in Power BI:

Consider a multinational organization operating in the European Union (EU), which must adhere to the General Data Protection Regulation (GDPR). Using Power BI, they classify and apply sensitivity labels to different datasets, design data lineage to trace data sources, and configure role-level security to restrict access. This ensures that personal data is protected, and access is granted only to authorized personnel. Power BI's audit logs provide evidence for compliance with GDPR regulations.

The Evolving Landscape of Data Governance:

Data governance will continue to evolve as new regulations and data management challenges emerge. Power BI is committed to adapting to these changes, offering enhanced data governance features and integrations to support evolving data management needs.

By focusing on data governance and compliance, organizations can navigate complex data landscapes while maintaining the highest standards of data quality and security.

21.2. Data Security and Privacy

In today's data-driven world, safeguarding data security and privacy is paramount. As organizations collect and analyze increasing volumes of data, the risk of data breaches and privacy violations also grows. Power BI provides robust features to help organizations secure their data and ensure compliance with privacy regulations, such as GDPR, HIPAA, or CCPA.

The Importance of Data Security and Privacy:

Data security and privacy are crucial for maintaining the trust of customers, partners, and regulators. Breaches can lead to legal consequences, financial penalties, and reputational damage. Organizations must prioritize protecting sensitive information to avoid these risks.

Key Aspects of Data Security and Privacy in Power BI:

Power BI offers several features and best practices to enhance data security and privacy:

1. Encryption: Power BI ensures data encryption both in transit and at rest. This includes secure connections and encryption mechanisms to protect data from unauthorized access.

2. Row-Level Security: Implementing row-level security in Power BI allows organizations to restrict data access based on user roles. This ensures that only authorized personnel can see specific data.

3. Data Loss Prevention (DLP): Power BI integrates with Microsoft 365's DLP policies, allowing organizations to prevent data leaks by defining policies that govern data sharing and access.

4. Sensitivity Labels: Sensitivity labels can be applied to classify data, specifying its sensitivity level. This labeling helps in controlling access and sharing based on the data's classification.

5. Privacy Level Settings: Power BI provides privacy level settings during data source connection, ensuring that data from different sources is handled according to its privacy requirements.

Example: GDPR Compliance with Power BI:

Consider an e-commerce company operating globally, including in the European Union (EU), where they must adhere to GDPR. To comply with GDPR's data privacy requirements, they classify customer data as sensitive, apply sensitivity labels, and implement row-level security. This ensures that personal data is protected, and only authorized employees can access it. Furthermore, they configure privacy level settings to govern data flow and comply with GDPR's data protection mandates.

Future of Data Security and Privacy:

Data security and privacy will continue to be at the forefront of data modeling, as more regulations emerge and the value of personal and sensitive data grows. Power BI is committed to evolving to meet these challenges, providing enhanced security and privacy features.

21.3. Collaboration and Data Sharing

In the rapidly evolving landscape of data modeling, collaboration and data sharing are becoming increasingly essential. Modern businesses and organizations no longer operate in isolation. They rely on effective collaboration and data sharing to make informed decisions, drive innovation, and stay competitive. Power BI offers a variety of features and strategies to enable seamless collaboration and secure data sharing.

The Significance of Collaboration and Data Sharing:

1. *Foster Innovation:* Collaboration allows teams to work together, share insights, and come up with innovative solutions. This collaborative approach leads to better decision-making and problem-solving.

2. *Cross-Functional Insights:* Different departments within an organization can benefit from each other's data. Data sharing breaks down silos, providing a holistic view of the business's performance.

3. *External Partnerships:* Businesses often need to share data with external partners, such as suppliers or clients. Secure data sharing is crucial for these relationships.

Key Aspects of Collaboration and Data Sharing in Power BI:

1. Workspace Collaboration: Power BI workspaces provide a shared environment for teams to collaborate on reports and dashboards. Users can collaborate on the same dataset, create reports, and share insights.

2. Collaboration Tools: Integration with Microsoft Teams and SharePoint allows for seamless collaboration. Users can share reports and dashboards directly in Teams, facilitating discussions around data insights.

3. Publish to Web: Power BI offers a "Publish to web" feature for public data sharing. Users can generate an embed code and share dashboards with a wider audience, even if they don't have a Power BI account.

4. Row-Level Security: Organizations can use row-level security to control what data specific users or groups can access. This is particularly useful when sharing sensitive information internally.

Example: Collaborative Sales Reporting:

Imagine a sales team using Power BI for reporting and analytics. They have created sales reports and share them within their Power BI workspace. The sales manager uses Power BI's collaboration features to invite team members, share insights, and discuss strategies. They can also use "Publish to web" to share a sales dashboard with external partners and embed it on the company website, providing clients with real-time data insights.

The Future of Collaboration and Data Sharing:

The future of data modeling is closely intertwined with collaboration and data sharing. As organizations continue to embrace remote work and global partnerships, efficient collaboration and secure data sharing will be vital for decision-making and growth. Power BI will continue to enhance its features to meet these emerging needs.

CHAPTER IX
Supplementary Materials

Part.22 Appendix A: DAX Function Reference

22.1. DAX Function Categories

Data Analysis Expressions (DAX) functions are the building blocks of Power BI, enabling users to create powerful calculations and transformations in their data models. These functions can be categorized into several distinct groups based on their primary use cases. Understanding these categories is crucial for mastering DAX and leveraging it effectively for your data modeling needs.

Common DAX Function Categories:

1. Math and Trigonometry Functions:

   - These functions encompass mathematical operations like addition, subtraction, multiplication, and trigonometric operations such as sine and cosine.

   - *Example*: The `SUMX` function falls into this category as it's used for summation.

2. Date and Time Functions:

   - Date and time functions help you manipulate and analyze date and time values. They are essential for time-based analyses.

   - *Example*: The `DATEADD` function allows you to add or subtract a specific time period from a date.

3. Filter Functions:

- These functions allow you to filter data based on specific conditions, returning subsets of data that meet the criteria.

- *Example*: The `FILTER` function is used to create filtered tables based on defined conditions.

4. Information Functions:

- Information functions provide details about the data model and its structure.

- *Example*: The `ISBLANK` function checks if a value is blank or null.

5. Text Functions:

- Text functions help manipulate and analyze text data within your model. They can be used for tasks like text extraction, concatenation, and formatting.

- *Example*: The `CONCATENATE` function combines text values.

6. Statistical Functions:

- Statistical functions perform statistical calculations on data, including mean, median, and standard deviation.

- *Example*: The `AVERAGE` function calculates the average of a column of numeric values.

7. Information Functions:

- These functions provide details about the data model and its structure.

- *Example*: The `ISBLANK` function checks if a value is blank or null.

8. Time Intelligence Functions:

- Time intelligence functions enable advanced date calculations for creating reports with a time dimension.

    - *Example*: The `TOTALYTD` function calculates the total year-to-date value.

9. Aggregate Functions:

    - Aggregate functions help summarize data by returning aggregated values from a table or column.

    - *Example*: The `SUMMARIZE` function generates summary tables with aggregated data.

Using DAX Function Categories:

Understanding DAX function categories is vital because it allows you to select the right function for the task at hand. For example, when you need to perform mathematical calculations on your data, you'll know to look within the Math and Trigonometry category. When working with dates and time, you'll turn to the Date and Time functions.

In this appendix, we'll delve into each category in detail, providing a comprehensive overview of the functions within it and illustrating their usage with practical examples.

Conclusion:

DAX functions are a powerful feature of Power BI, and organizing them into categories based on their functionality makes them more accessible and understandable for users. This section introduces readers to the primary DAX function categories, offering a glimpse of the diverse capabilities DAX provides for advanced data modeling.

22.2. DAX Function Syntax and Usage

Data Analysis Expressions (DAX) functions are the heart of Power BI's data modeling capabilities. They allow users to create complex calculations, manipulate data, and perform a wide range of operations. Understanding the syntax and usage of DAX functions is crucial for harnessing their power effectively. In this section, we'll explore the syntax and usage of DAX functions in detail.

DAX Function Syntax:

Every DAX function follows a specific syntax. While the syntax may vary from function to function, there are common elements:

1. Function Name: The name of the DAX function you want to use.

2. Arguments: Arguments are inputs required by the function to perform its operation. They are enclosed within parentheses and separated by commas. The number and type of arguments can vary from one function to another.

3. Result: The result is the output of the function's operation, which can be a single value, a table, or a table of values.

Example of DAX Function Syntax:

Let's take the `SUMX` function as an example. Its syntax is as follows:

```DAX
SUMX(<table>, <expression>)
```

- Function Name: SUMX

- Arguments: It requires two arguments:

  - `<table>`: The table or table expression to iterate over.

  - `<expression>`: The expression to evaluate for each row of the table.

- Result: The result is a scalar value, which is the sum of the expression for each row in the table.

DAX Function Usage:

DAX functions serve various purposes, from simple arithmetic operations to complex aggregations and time-based calculations. Here are some common scenarios and their corresponding DAX functions:

1. Simple Aggregation:

   - Scenario: Calculate the total sales for a specific product category.

   - DAX Function: `SUMX`, `FILTER`

   Usage Example:

   ```DAX

   Total Sales = SUMX(FILTER(Sales, Sales[Category] = "Electronics"), Sales[Amount])

   ```


2. Time Intelligence:

   - Scenario: Calculate the year-to-date sales for a specific product.

- DAX Function: `TOTALYTD`

Usage Example:

```DAX
YTD Sales = TOTALYTD(SUM(Sales[Amount]), 'Date'[Date])
```

3. Ranking and Top N:

   - Scenario: Find the top-selling products.

   - DAX Function: `TOPN`

Usage Example:

```DAX
Top Selling Products = TOPN(10, Sales, Sales[Amount])
```

4. Text Manipulation:

   - Scenario: Concatenate text values for reporting.

   - DAX Function: `CONCATENATEX`

Usage Example:

```DAX
Product List = CONCATENATEX(Products, Products[Product Name], ", ")
```

Conclusion:

Understanding the syntax and usage of DAX functions empowers users to create advanced calculations and unlock the full potential of Power BI. By providing real-world usage examples and demystifying DAX function syntax, this section equips readers with the knowledge they need to become proficient DAX users.

Part 23. Appendix B: Sample Datasets and Exercises

23.1. Sample Datasets for Practice

In the journey of mastering Data Analysis Expressions (DAX) and advanced data modeling in Power BI, hands-on practice with real-world datasets is invaluable. This section provides a curated collection of sample datasets designed to help you build your DAX skills and gain practical experience. Each dataset is accompanied by a brief description and suggestions for exercises to apply your DAX knowledge.

1. Sales and Product Data:

Description: This dataset contains information about sales transactions, product details, customer demographics, and dates. It's an ideal starting point for practicing basic DAX calculations like summing sales, calculating profit margins, and identifying top-selling products.

Exercise Suggestions:

- Calculate the total sales for each product category.

- Determine the profit margin for each sale.

- Find the top-selling products for the last quarter.

2. Employee and HR Data:

Description: This dataset includes employee records with attributes such as employee ID, hire date, department, and performance metrics. It's suitable for practicing DAX functions related to employee performance analysis, time-based calculations, and HR analytics.

Exercise Suggestions:

- Calculate employee tenure in years.

- Determine the average performance rating by department.

- Identify employees with the highest sales performance in the last year.

3. Financial and Stock Market Data:

Description: This dataset contains historical financial data, including stock prices, trading volumes, and company financials. It's excellent for advanced DAX exercises involving time intelligence functions, financial calculations, and stock market analytics.

Exercise Suggestions:

- Calculate moving averages for stock prices.

- Determine the highest trading volume day for each stock.

- Analyze the correlation between stock prices and company revenue.

4. E-commerce Customer Data:

Description: This dataset comprises customer profiles, purchase history, and website interaction data. It's ideal for practicing DAX functions related to customer segmentation, cohort analysis, and website performance tracking.

Exercise Suggestions:

- Segment customers based on purchase behavior.

- Analyze customer retention over time.

- Calculate website conversion rates for different products.

5. Healthcare Patient Records:

Description: This dataset contains anonymized patient records with attributes such as diagnoses, treatments, and patient demographics. It's suitable for healthcare analytics and DAX exercises related to patient outcomes, cost analysis, and clinical trial data.

Exercise Suggestions:

- Analyze the average length of hospital stays by diagnosis.

- Calculate the cost of treatment for different patient groups.

- Identify trends in clinical trial participation over time.

These sample datasets are available for download and use in your Power BI projects. By working through the exercises and applying DAX functions to real data, you'll enhance your skills and gain a deeper understanding of data modeling and analysis.

23.2. Exercise Solutions and Walkthroughs

This section provides comprehensive solutions and step-by-step walkthroughs for the exercises presented in "23.1. Sample Datasets for Practice." It serves as a practical guide for readers to check their work, learn different problem-solving techniques, and deepen their understanding of DAX and data modeling.

Exercise 1: Calculating Total Sales by Product Category

Solution:

To calculate the total sales by product category, we'll use the following DAX expression in Power BI:

```DAX
Total Sales by Product Category = SUMX(Sales, Sales[Sales Amount])
```

Walkthrough:

1. Open your Power BI file.

2. Create a new measure by going to "Modeling" in the Power BI Desktop and selecting "New Measure."

3. Enter the DAX expression above and give your measure an appropriate name (e.g., Total Sales by Product Category).

4. Now, create a visualization, such as a bar chart, and add the "Product Category" dimension to the axis and the "Total Sales by Product Category" measure to the values.

5. You should see a bar chart that displays the total sales for each product category.

Exercise 2: Determining Employee Tenure in Years

Solution:

To calculate employee tenure in years, we can use the following DAX expression:

```DAX
Employee Tenure (Years) = DATEDIFF(Employees[Hire Date], TODAY(), YEAR)
```

Walkthrough:

1. Create a new measure in Power BI as explained earlier.

2. Enter the DAX expression mentioned above and give your measure an appropriate name (e.g., Employee Tenure in Years).

3. Next, create a table visualization and add the "Employee Name" or any relevant identifier to the columns, along with the "Employee Tenure in Years" measure.

4. This table will display employee names alongside their tenure in years.

Exercise 3: Calculating Moving Averages for Stock Prices

Solution:

To calculate moving averages for stock prices, you can use DAX functions like AVERAGEX and FILTER. Here's an example for a 30-day moving average:

```DAX
30-Day Moving Average =
AVERAGEX(
    FILTER('Stock Data', 'Stock Data'[Date] >= EARLIER('Stock Data'[Date]) - 29 && 'Stock Data'[Date] <= EARLIER('Stock Data'[Date])),
    'Stock Data'[Price]
```

)

```

Walkthrough:

1. Create a new measure, just like before.

2. Enter the DAX expression for your desired moving average (e.g., 30-Day Moving Average).

3. In a line chart or area chart, place the "Date" on the axis and your moving average measure in the values field.

4. You will visualize the stock price trend with a 30-day moving average line.

By following these solutions and walkthroughs, readers can gain hands-on experience with DAX and Power BI, improving their data modeling and analysis skills. It's important to encourage readers to attempt the exercises themselves before referring to the solutions to maximize the learning experience.
```

Part 24. Appendix C: Notes and Glossary

24.1. Key Concepts and Definitions

In this section, we'll explore essential concepts and definitions that are fundamental to mastering DAX and advanced data modeling in Power BI. These key terms and ideas form the foundation of your understanding and proficiency in using Power BI effectively.

Data Modeling: Data modeling is the process of creating a visual representation of data to understand, analyze, and gain insights. In Power BI, data modeling involves defining relationships between tables, creating calculated columns, measures, and optimizing the data structure for efficient analysis.

DAX (Data Analysis Expressions): DAX is a powerful formula language used for creating custom calculations in Power BI. It's designed for data analysis and allows you to create complex calculations, such as aggregations, calculations based on filters, and time intelligence functions.

Tables: In Power BI, tables represent structured datasets. They consist of rows and columns, with each row representing a specific record, and each column representing a field or attribute.

Columns: Columns in Power BI tables are used to store data attributes. These can include numerical values, text, dates, or any data type relevant to your analysis.

Measures: Measures are calculated values based on DAX expressions. They allow you to perform aggregations, calculations, and create key performance indicators (KPIs). Measures are typically used for values that need to change dynamically in response to user interactions.

Calculated Columns: Calculated columns are columns within a table that are created by defining a DAX formula. They can be used to extend the data model by adding new columns based on existing data.

Relationships: Relationships define how tables are related to each other. In Power BI, you can create relationships between tables to establish connections that allow for cross-filtering and data exploration.

Filter Context: Filter context refers to the set of filters applied to data when performing calculations. It's essential for understanding how DAX calculations are affected by filter selections in Power BI reports.

Row Context: Row context occurs when DAX formulas are applied at a row level, allowing you to create calculations that depend on individual rows in a table.

Time Intelligence Functions: Time intelligence functions in DAX enable you to perform calculations based on time-related attributes. This is crucial for tasks such as year-to-date calculations, rolling averages, and comparing data over different time periods.

Normalization: Data normalization is the process of organizing data into structured tables with minimal data redundancy. It helps reduce data errors, improve data integrity, and optimize storage.

Cardinality: Cardinality refers to the type and number of relationships between tables. Understanding the cardinality of relationships is essential for effective data modeling.

Star Schema: A star schema is a data modeling technique where one central fact table is connected to dimension tables. It's a common schema for creating data models in Power BI.

Snowflake Schema: The snowflake schema is an extension of the star schema where dimension tables are further normalized into multiple related tables. It's useful for complex data models with many attributes.

Granularity: Granularity defines the level of detail in data. It's important to choose the right level of granularity to ensure accurate analysis.

Example: Suppose you have a sales dataset with tables for sales, products, and customers. In this scenario, the "Sales Amount" column in the sales table is a measure that calculates the total sales. "Product Name" and "Customer Name" are examples of columns that store attributes, and "Date" is used for time intelligence functions.

These key concepts and definitions serve as the building blocks for advanced data modeling in Power BI. A solid grasp of these terms will greatly enhance your ability to create insightful reports and dashboards in Power BI.

CONCLUSION

In conclusion, "Power BI: Mastering DAX for Advanced Data Modeling" has taken you on a comprehensive journey through the world of data modeling and analysis. We've explored the intricacies of DAX, delved into advanced techniques for transforming data into insights, and discovered the powerful capabilities of Power BI.

Throughout this book, you've learned how to build robust data models, create meaningful visualizations, and make data-driven decisions that can shape the future of your organization. We've covered a wide range of topics, from the fundamentals of DAX to handling large datasets, advanced case studies, and future trends in data modeling.

As you now close this book, we hope you're leaving with a deeper understanding of the potential that Power BI and DAX offer. The skills and knowledge you've gained are not just tools; they are keys to unlocking the true value of data and using it to drive success in your professional endeavors.

Thank you for choosing "Power BI: Mastering DAX for Advanced Data Modeling" as your guide. We appreciate your dedication to advancing your skills and knowledge in the field of data analysis and business intelligence. We wish you the utmost success in your data modeling endeavors and look forward to your continued journey in the world of data.

We would like to express our heartfelt gratitude to each and every reader who has chosen to embark on this educational journey with us. Your support and trust in our book are what drive us to continue creating resources that empower you to excel in the field of data analysis.

We would also like to thank you for investing your valuable time and effort in mastering DAX and Power BI. As you apply the knowledge gained from this book to real-world projects and scenarios, you're not only advancing your own career but also contributing to the broader field of data analysis and business intelligence.

We hope you find this book an essential asset in your professional growth, and we look forward to providing you with more valuable resources in the future. Once again, thank you for choosing **"Power BI: Mastering DAX for Advanced Data Modeling."**